Fiona O'Loughlin is Australian comedy royalty with an award-winning career of almost twenty years. Fiona performs to packed houses across the globe, from headlining the world-renowned Improv comedy club in LA, to repeat seasons in Hong Kong, and performing at Edinburgh Festival Fringe, Montreal's 'Just For Laughs' comedy festival, the UK's Leicester Comedy Festival, Adelaide Fringe and the Melbourne International Comedy Festival.

As well as a critically acclaimed stand-up comedian, Fiona is an accomplished author, publishing *Me of the Never Never* in 2011. She has also appeared on *I'm a Celebrity ... Get Me Out of Here!*, *Good News Week*, *Spicks and Specks* and *Celebrity Apprentice* among many other television shows. Fiona lives in Adelaide.

TRUTHS FROM AN UNRELIABLE WITNESS

A MEMOIR

FIONA O'LOUGHLIN

With Alley Pascoe

hachette
AUSTRALIA

PUBLISHER'S NOTE: This very honest memoir at times contains what could be distressing descriptions of addiction and discussions of mental health crises.

If you are affected by any of the content, please refer to the resources page at the back of the book for support service information.

Some pseudonyms have been used in this book and other details altered where necessary to protect the identity and privacy of people mentioned.

Lyrics from 'The Loving Time', written by Noel Brazil, on pages 111–12 reproduced with permission by Joseph O'Reilly, Little Rox Music.

 hachette
AUSTRALIA

Published in Australia and New Zealand in 2020
by Hachette Australia
(an imprint of Hachette Australia Pty Limited)
Level 17, 207 Kent Street, Sydney NSW 2000
www.hachette.com.au

10 9 8 7 6 5 4 3 2 1

Copyright © Fiona O'Loughlin 2020

 A catalogue record for this
book is available from the
NATIONAL
LIBRARY National Library of Australia
OF AUSTRALIA

ISBN: 978 0 7336 4570 9 (paperback)

Cover design by Christabella Designs
Cover photograph courtesy of Fiona O'Loughlin
Typeset in Adobe Garamond Pro by Kirby Jones
Printed and bound in Great Britain by Clays Ltd, Elcograf S.p.A.

To my parents, Deirdre and Denis

CONTENTS

A NOTE TO THE READER

'There are three sides to every story: my side, your side, and the truth. And no one is lying. Memories shared serve each one differently.' – **Robert Evans**

MY CHILDHOOD NICKNAME WAS 'FORGETFUL FI'. I'VE never had a mind for dates, I've lost every wallet I've owned and I couldn't tell you where my birth certificate is, but I can still see the delicate face of my first baby the day he was born, thirty-four years ago. I can remember the lines of my dad's hard-working hands, the scent of my childhood bedroom and the all-consuming guilt of waking up hungover in a shabby motel with a heavy blue quilt on top of me and a hard pillow underneath my head; but after a life of heavy drinking and a fifteen-day coma, my memories have blurred into one glorious and intense scrapbook without page numbers or any semblance of a timeline. I am an unreliable witness to my own life.

This book is a record of moments, events and experiences that have humoured, humbled and heartbroken me, but it is not an actual book of record. Writing these pages, I've searched my mind for clarity to tell my story as I remember it. Others will recall the story differently. But this is my book (get your own). It may not always be accurate – but it is all true.

SCREAMING INTO THE VOID

I T'S NOT THE FIRST TIME I'VE HIT ROCK BOTTOM, AND IT won't be the last.

It looks different this time, though: darker, harsher, absolute. I realise I'm in more danger than I've ever been in. I can feel the peril in the back of my throat, but I swallow it down, like the burning tears of my childhood. A few months earlier, I was released from a psychiatric ward after being in a coma in hospital for a little over two weeks. Now, I'm living in a share house in suburban Adelaide with a healer who has stepped in to save me. Except, the share house is a drug den. I'm not sure if she's saving me or manipulating me. New friends drop by to say g'day. Except, the friends are meth addicts scoring gear at all hours of the day and night from my fellow housemates. I hear small talk between my housemates and their guests. Except, the small talk is hushed voices discussing knocking people off and stolen goods. A pet rabbit joyfully roams through the house. Except it's not a pet. It's a lost soul like the rest of us, trapped by four walls of despair. There is no joy.

The house is stunningly stark. It's hopeless. I'm hopeless. I'm in the throes of relapse. I don't recognise myself in the mirror. I'm skin and bone, scrounging through my purse to buy mini bottles of vodka instead of food, surviving off parcels left on my doorstep by a friend smart enough not to give me money for groceries.

I take a puff of the meth pipe handed to me and I feel numb. I'm in the bleakest place I've ever been, and I'm not scared. I'm nothing. It's like I'm floating. I immediately understand that meth is a dangerous dance partner and I don't seek it out, but I do accept its hand when it's offered to me, ushering me onto the dance floor with its arm wrapped tightly around my waist, waltz ready.

Every morning I wake up in my windowless bedroom, empty but for the cupboard in the corner. I shake the rabbit shit out of my boots and pull them on. A painting hangs on the wall. It's a black-and-white abstract portrait of a woman in agony, pure hell. For a second, I wonder if I'm looking into a mirror. I walk up to her, look her in the eye and mime a scream, 'Morning!' pretending I'm completely normal, just saying hi to my friend. I laugh at my own absurdity. It's a daily ritual. A reminder that I know how dire my life has become. A last straw of sanity.

Very few people know I'm here. I've gone underground. There's nowhere else to go. I don't want my family or my kids to see me like this. The shame would kill me before the alcohol, before the meth, before the malnutrition. I am the walking dead. I know there are only three ways this ends: institution, jail or death.

How did I get here? I ask. I cry. I scream at the painting.

A SEAT AT THE TABLE

MY LIFE STORY CAN BE TRACED THROUGH DINNER tables, the grain of the wood interrupted by imperfect knots marking milestones and mistakes. In my childhood home in the small town of Warooka on South Australia's Yorke Peninsula, I had to fight for a seat at the kitchen table where my mum and dad raised seven kids: Genevieve, Richard, me, Catherine (Cate), Justin, Sarah and finally little Emily Brigid. The Taheny kids. Our kitchen never seemed large enough for nine people.

For such a big family, the silence around the kitchen table at dinner time was deafening. I was a happy enough child, though prone to bouts of melancholia. I felt trapped in an era when kids didn't have a voice. I hated the rigidity, rules and monotony of childhood. Mum was flat out cooking, cleaning and looking after kids and Dad was flat out farming. There wasn't a lot of time for childlike glee. Adults always seemed to be saying, 'Okay, that's enough fun for now.' I begged to differ; there was never enough fun. I couldn't wait to grow up, get married and laugh every day, loud and obnoxiously.

The extent of our mealtime conversation was Mum calling out, 'Come and get your dinner while it's hot.' It was sit down, shut up, eat. The sound of chewing and butter knives scraping across ceramic plates nearly sent me mad. I desperately wanted dinner time to be like it was in those American sitcoms on the telly, with everyone talking about their day, passing anecdotes around the table like salt and pepper. It wasn't. No one ever said 'I love you' in our household, or any other household that I knew. It just wasn't the done thing. We were still a generation away from validated feelings, public displays of affection and heartfelt declarations.

I secretly dreamed of being an actress in one of those sitcoms, but I never dared say that out loud. Back then, the worst thing you could be was full of yourself. You could be talented, sure, but you were never allowed to show off. It was a tricky tightrope to walk as a kid, and I'm not sure I ever mastered the skill.

My parents, Deirdre and Denis, were of the silent generation; stoic and rarely openly emotional. Mum's dad died when she was three, so she was raised by a single mother and moved about from place to place. Mum doesn't complain about her childhood. Her unofficial philosophy for life is, 'Just get on with it.' When I think about what she might have gone through, I understand that sometimes words are safer left unspoken.

One thing we definitely didn't speak about back then was sex. In St Brigid's church, where we always sat as a family in the very front row on the left singing hymns such as 'Faith of Our Fathers', 'Sweet Sacrament Divine' and 'We Stand for God and for His Glory', I was taught that sex was forbidden and would earn you a one-way ticket to hell. When I got my period, I used only pads and worried about friends who tempted Satan with tampons. I shut down the sexual part of myself altogether as soon as I hit puberty; it was like I emotionally circumcised myself. To this day I have never masturbated or had an orgasm.

I had my first kiss at age thirteen, when a grown-up visitor came into the bathroom while I was brushing my teeth before bed. He locked the door behind him and shoved his tongue in my mouth. I froze. It was shockingly grotesque, like stepping on a slug barefoot. Mum had cooked beef stroganoff and pasta for dinner that night and the house still smelled of sautéed onion and mushroom when I ran to my bedroom. I didn't know what had just happened to me, but I knew that I could never tell anyone about it. I wouldn't have had the language to explain what happened even if I wanted to. Sometimes words are safer left unspoken.

I don't know what was worse in the Taheny household: the silence or the yelling. My mum was short fused. All adults seemed short fused then. I don't know anyone my age who escaped their childhood free of scars from emotional, physical or sexual abuse. Violence always seemed to bubble under the surface in the 1970s. Every time it spilled over, the back of my throat would burn with tears. My stomach would turn and tighten at the hint of raised voices. It still does. I hated being yelled at – and seeing my brothers and sisters in trouble – so I took on the responsibility of being the clown of the house and the classroom, desperate to break the tension and make everything okay. When my siblings and cousins were hit with wooden spoons at home and belted with leather straps at school by the nuns, I felt their pain. Our school motto was, 'What happens at school stays at school, what happens at home stays at home.' The silence and the violence were intrinsically connected, like an infinity symbol of suffering. Still to this day, I can't stand other people's hurt. It's intolerable to me and I'll do anything to fix it.

Contradictorily, one of my happiest childhood memories happened at our strictly regulated kitchen table. I was thirteen. In the adjoining living room at Warooka the theme song from M*A*S*H was just beginning, and the warm, sweet smell of a summer breeze hand in hand with daylight savings wafted through the sunroom, knocking on the screen door like a favourite cousin coming for a sleepover. We had a cold collation for dinner that night: leftover corned beef, beetroot, chicken wings, potato salad and button mushrooms from a can. Mum was, and still is, a first-rate cook and would never have fashioned such a graceless meal, but she had not long had her seventh baby and I was chef that night. My first culinary effort – and everybody ate it.

I don't know why that is one of my happiest memories, but I guess I felt useful. I have never eaten a button mushroom or heard the theme song from M*A*S*H since without a sense of happy recall. Unlike beef stroganoff.

Even though they didn't voice it, Mum's and Dad's love for us was absolute. I recall them being very tactile when we were little. I remember Dad rubbing us with towels after bath time with squeal-inducing vigour, warm flannelette pyjamas that always matched and Mum's comfort food: especially her golden-syrup dumplings. No doubt about it, I knew I was loved. Sometimes words don't need to be spoken to be felt.

Our quiet kitchen table transformed whenever we had guests over. As a large Catholic family, Mum and Dad had a lot of funny friends and relations, and my parents were incredibly hospitable. Everyone would come back to our place after last call at the Warooka Hotel on the weekend. We'd sit around the table telling stories, making each other laugh and impersonating all and sundry. In a way, I started my apprenticeship in stand-up comedy around that cramped kitchen table, sitting on a piano stool because we'd run out of dining chairs. As a kid, I watched and listened to the storyteller – and the audience. I didn't have much to say until I got older.

My seat at the kitchen table completely changed as soon as I turned eighteen. It was like I graduated to adulthood and my prize was the banter and levity I'd always dreamed of. I found an instinct for the rhythm of stories and I could tell when someone's anecdote was about to go belly up.

I remember being as young as ten and thinking if Aunty Pat had just told the story about the dead kitten differently, she would have got a bigger laugh. She should have started out with the bad smell coming from the car and not given away the bit about the fur under the bonnet until the end.

My favourite stories were from Dad reliving his childhood. I recognised great comic timing in my dad at a very early age, and yet he was regarded as the quiet one out of him and Mum.

I was furious the day I came home from my public school after learning about evolution for the first time in Year 8 science.

'Dad? How come nobody ever told me we came from apes?'

He didn't even look up from the *Stock Journal* he was reading. 'Well, you can speak for yourself.'

*

When I was nineteen, I was introduced to an entirely different dinner table – in the O'Loughlins' home in the Adelaide suburb of Glengowrie. I'd met Christopher O'Loughlin at the Queen's Head Hotel in North Adelaide after we'd run in similar circles all our lives. At the time, I was working as a nurse's aide and living in a share house, having graduated from Cabra College with pretty average grades and no real life plan except to be independent and free. I spent an ungodly amount of time thinking about Chris O'Loughlin, whom I'd been admiring from afar at gatherings with mutual friends. He was desperately handsome, and I was desperately smitten.

Chris was also one of seven. His family was every bit as close as mine – and I grew to love them every bit as much as mine. Chris's mum, Geraldine, and younger sister Libby had been killed in a plane crash in 1980 on their way back to Adelaide from Alice Springs, leaving behind his father, Ivan, and siblings Justin, Genevieve, Peter, Tim and Jude. Serendipitously, I was one of fourteen students from my boarding school in Adelaide to form a guard of honour for their funeral at Our Lady of Victories Church in Glenelg. That was where I first laid eyes on Chris – not that we met that day, but it still created a special bond in our relationship. I'm forever grateful that I was able to pay a small tribute to the mother-in-law and sister-in-law I would never know. I remember asking Chris about his mum and trying to paint a picture of her in my mind. He adored her.

'What was she like?' I would ask.

'She loved to laugh. I remember she would sit on the phone for hours chatting and chain-smoking. And she'd do silly dances when she did the ironing,' Chris told me. She sounded like pure bliss to me. We sure could have done with some silly dancing in Warooka growing up. I started talking to Geraldine, telling her my worries, hopes and fears.

At first, I was bewildered by the O'Loughlin dinner table. Their conversation could turn instantaneously into the fiercest arguments I'd ever heard. Politics, art, religion: they were programmed to be devil's advocate to each other and then in a split-second someone, usually Chris's brother Tim, would say something hysterical and they'd collapse with laughter. I remember sitting at the table one night in those early days and realising what made this kitchen table so different from my own. This was an uncensored table. Just about any subject was up for grabs and language was as free flowing as the wine.

The O'Loughlins had a proud history as pioneers of Irish music in Australia. They were quick to pull out a guitar around the family table, and even quicker to belt out a tune. With a chorus of uncles and aunts, they'd sing Latin carols in three-part harmonies. Their Christmas tradition was to gather around the piano and make sweet, sweet music together. My life story can be told through dinner tables and the songs sung in the early hours of the morning, like ballads that make your heart swell and your eyes well.

*

In 1985, a week after our wedding, Chris and I both swapped our family dinner tables for a second-hand fold-down table in our first house, on Newland Street in Alice Springs, where Chris worked as a dental technician. Having grown up in a Catholic, politically right-wing household, Alice Springs was my New York. Seeing the red centre for the first time really is remarkable. The first thing that smacks you in the face when you drive through the MacDonnell Ranges is the colour of the sky: cloudless and blue. The blue feels brighter than anywhere else, contrasted against the rich red dirt. Introducing your eyes to Alice Springs is like finally putting on those reading glasses that you've needed for a while; everything looks clearer, sharper.

Chris's brother Justin had given us a bric-à-brac wooden table with four matching chairs, and they were my most prized possession. In the early days when Chris was at work and I was home alone, I used to cling to that little table as it was the only aesthetically pleasing thing in the house. It used to fold down to a half-circle, and every day I would rearrange what was on it – flowers, a fruit bowl, crockery. I was playing house, I guess, but it never took me long, because that table was the only thing I had to work with, at first. Less than a year into our marriage, we set up a highchair around the bric-à-brac table for our first son, Henry, who was born in 1986, then again for Brigid (Biddy) in 1988 and once more for Tess in 1989. If three kids under three wasn't manic enough, we also started fostering in 1990, taking in emergency short-term placements. Our first charge was a one-year-old Aboriginal boy called Terence who came to us on weekends and holidays for a couple of years to give his primary foster carers a break. He was a magnificent baby and every one of us fell in love with him on sight. His marshmallow cheeks were as soft as his hair and he was little for his age, but as brave as a ten-year-old.

Terence had been born so premature that he didn't have the sucking mechanism that babies instinctively have. Up until he was two years old, he was fed solely by a gastrostomy tube: we had to attach a funnel to the tube every mealtime and pour a bottle of milk directly into his stomach. Still, when he saw the bottle coming, he'd kick his little legs with the same excitement as a baby who was actually going to taste the milk. Without the tube, Terence wouldn't have been able to survive. He had a younger sister in Adelaide who was born even more premature than him and would never walk or talk, and it was at this baby's birth that Terence's mother had died.

One of the saddest and happiest days with him was the day he had his gastrostomy tube removed as a toddler. He was with us at the time because he was between permanent homes. Having his tube removed meant that he was now able to live with his relations safely in a bush community and would not be coming to us anymore. To this day I have never laid eyes on that gorgeous little boy again.

I believe our family wouldn't be who we are today if it hadn't been for Terence. I've never loved a foster baby more than I loved him. In fact, I ended up loving him as much as my own kids. Looking after Terence was one of the most emotionally peaceful times in my life. When I was fostering, I took myself off the hook for all my other sins. The peace it afforded me was amazing. It's a cliché, but we really did get as much out of it as the foster kids did. I thrived on the chaos, and my philosophy was 'the more the merrier'.

We moved into our family home in the Old Eastside of Alice Springs in 1992 with three kids, and went on to have Albert (Bert) and Mary-Agnes, plus a stream of foster kids, including Mitch, who came to us as a two-year-old after his mother abandoned him. Out of all the kids we took care of, Mitch broke my heart the most. Growing up without a mother's love left him hardened on the inside. He was unused to being hugged or kissed and reminded me of a burly truckie trapped in a baby's body. It took Mitch a long time to let his guard down with us, but by the time he left us after four months to live with his newly discovered aunt in Queensland, Mitch was one of us. It was hard to let him go, but that's how fostering works.

To accommodate our growing family and our ring-ins, we upgraded the bric-à-brac table to a heavy wooden dining set, stretching long enough to fit twelve chairs. The house was rambling and horse-shoe-shaped with a courtyard in the middle, high ceilings inside, cement floors, white walls and French doors. I loved it.

Inside was a hive of mayhem otherwise known as 'the land of do as you please'. I was determined to drown out the silence of my childhood. We never had formal family dinners; I'd eat standing up or watching TV on the couch. To have a sit-down dinner, when I had hated them so much as a kid, would have felt like a betrayal of myself. I still didn't have the sitcom family dinner routine I dreamed of as a young girl, but at least I didn't have to listen to the sound of chewing and butter knives scraping ceramic plates.

When I wasn't filling the silence in the land of do as you please, I was doing it on stage and in print. I performed in a production of *Godspell* at Araluen Art Centre when I first moved to Alice and had emceed local cabarets over the years – even starring in a few of them. I also wrote a column for the local paper with musings on motherhood. Chris supported my extracurricular activities and my need to have a life and interests outside our home.

Our kitchen table was the place to be in Alice Springs. We'd have friends over on Friday nights and play cards until 3 am, spilling beer, singing songs and slapping our hands on the smooth wood with laughter. Chris and I were at our best when we were hosting company. We were united in wanting people to feel at home and have a good time at our place. We might not have had matching plates, but we knew how to have a laugh and enjoy ourselves. Whenever Chris pulled his guitar out, we'd sing Cat Stevens' 'How Can I Tell You' together … looking each other in the eye as we sang about not being able to find the words to say 'I love you'.

There was always music playing in our house and Chris had a broad ear. I remember him bringing home the new Mavericks album one Friday night with a carton of beer. We danced for the whole weekend. They were happy times, before I started drinking alone and first thing of a morning; before I lost control.

A welcome fixture at the table was my best friend, Jasmin, when she visited from Tennant Creek. We met at an all-girls boarding school, where we founded the NBK (Never Been Kissed) club and remained the closest of mates even after we graduated from the club and moved to our respective corners of the Northern Territory. Jasmin has taken in and raised many disadvantaged kids over the years and she's always had a sense of justice for the underdog. I remember going to the Big W near our boarding school as a teenager with Jasmin and our friend Mary-Anne to shop for toiletries. There was a woman in the same aisle as us, browsing deodorants as she merrily yelled at her young son and degraded him for all the store to hear. Jasmin let her have it. At sixteen, she squared off with the grown woman, shouting, 'Leave him alone, you mean old bitch.' I call Jasmin Mother Teresa – with a mouth like a sailor.

As the joke goes: Jasmin was staying with us in Alice Springs and went out to buy all the kids breakfast from McDonald's, a rare treat for her kids from Tennant Creek who didn't have the luxury of a Maccas in their town. Tragically, she arrived just after the 10.30 am breakfast cut-off and had to break the news to her son Ari, who was about six then, and small for his age. He immediately broke down in tears, so she scooped him up and cradled him in her arms, cooing soothing words and apologies, his head gently tucked into the nook of her collarbone, crying into the nape of her neck.

'You should have left earlier … you stupid cunt,' he wailed.

'I know, I know. I'm sorry,' she agreed. We all laughed until our sides hurt. Jasmin is the soul and conscience of our family.

Our kitchen table in Alice became the punchline of another of my most iconic jokes. On stage, I would dramatically lie on my side, re-enacting waking up with an awful hangover, with my husband asking me if I was getting up. 'No,' I'd say, with a quiver in my voice. 'I'm never getting up. I'm so embarrassed. I'm never, ever, *ever* getting up. This is my death bed.' And my husband would reply, 'Well, it may well be your death bed, but at the moment it's our kitchen table, and the kids need breakfast.' The crowd would laugh uproariously. From shows in New York to Montreal, Singapore to London and Edinburgh to Toronto, my kitchen-table gag never let me down. My life story can be traced through kitchen tables; beer stains soaked into the wood like spilled secrets and slurred conversations.

But this isn't that story. This is the story of table-less hotel rooms on the comedy circuit, smelling of dusty curtains and strewn with empty mini-bar vodka bottles. This is the story of a hospital tray, where I woke up after nearly dying from carbon monoxide poisoning. This is the story of a communal dining room in a rehab clinic that smelled of antiseptic and gravy. This is the story of a drug den in suburban Adelaide, where I hit rock bottom with a sickening thud, living in my own version of hell with meth addicts and a rabbit that shat through the entire house. My room didn't have a window, let alone a table.

I'm writing this story from my kitchen table in a tiny Adelaide rental apartment; a plain 1960s yellow-brick flat that feels like a heavenly oasis compared to the drug den. My small table is covered with a white tablecloth hiding the cheap wood veneer beneath it and I'm sipping on a lukewarm cup of English Breakfast tea. Once again, I'm playing house, arranging my furniture and filling vases with fresh flowers. The novelty of being an adult hasn't worn off yet. Adele's 'Turning Tables' is playing softly in the background.

My whole life, I've been fighting for my own nest, free from egg-shell silence and shattering screams. And after fifty-seven years, I've finally got it. My mother used to say, 'Well, you're very easily pleased,' as a backhanded compliment. When she visited me in my flat recently, she told me again, 'You really are easily pleased, and you always have been.' But she said it with love in her voice. I am a born optimist, if nothing else.

So, this is me. Content. Laying everything on the table (sorry, couldn't help myself). Please pull up a chair, you might want to sit down for this ...

CHAPTER 1

DROWNING IN THE DESERT

MY WEDDING DRESS WAS MADE OF TULLE. I LOOKED like one of those Kewpie dolls on a stick you'd buy from the Easter Show, but I felt every bit the beaming, blushing bride. I had pushed for the marriage. Well, to be honest, I had pushed for the wedding. I'd wanted a big, fun party, but I hadn't for a second considered the reality of being a wife. When the party ended, I moved to Alice Springs with someone I had never lived with. At least it was a bloody good party.

I'd lost my virginity to Chris when I was nineteen, after I got tired of saying no and knew he was the one. As a 'good' Catholic girl, I needed to marry him. For me, the night I first had sex was the night I committed to Chris forever. I lessened the shame I felt about having sex before marriage by 'doing the right thing'. I was only going to sleep with one person my whole life and that person was going to be Chris O'Loughlin. I hoped that by marrying the bloke, I wouldn't be sent to hell for my mortal sin.

I had been raised to fear hell. I remember a nun telling me, 'Hell is like a baby screaming for the mother it can never have.' It was a traumatic analogy, and one I thought of often. There were many elements to my religious upbringing and education that freaked me out. I'd lie awake at night worrying about those babies in limbo, the poor infants who had died before they'd been baptised and were subsequently disqualified from entering heaven and condemned to spend all of eternity floating about the atmosphere. I had never been able to get my head around the story of Jesus being nailed to a cross to atone for all of our sins. My mind could only ever focus on the brutality of a crucifixion death. Did he shift bearing weight from his feet to his hands? What an awful story. Religion had never once given me peace – only tortured visuals of those nails through bone and flesh, and haunting sounds of screaming babies. Even though part of me saw straight through the hypocrisy of the Catholic faith that spoke of love and harmony but taught shame and fear, I still didn't want to go to hell. I hate the heat.

My great-uncle was our parish priest for a time, and he conducted the Mass at our wedding. He was the brother of my mum's dad, the one who had died when she was three. Father John never invited us to call him uncle. He was so gruff and hard on us as kids, and I resented him for it, especially when I saw him being kind to other children. I never understood why he wasn't like that with us. We were his family, after all. Not them. Before my wedding, I boldly went into the confessional and said, 'Bless me, Father, for I have sinned. I've been having sex.' It was incredibly provocative of me. I figured, if you want to play the priest card, let's play the priest card. I can't remember what my penance was.

On my wedding day, Father John was especially cool to me. After the ceremony I thanked him for celebrating such a beautiful Mass, and he responded curtly, 'Every Mass is beautiful.' Noted.

When I picture that tulle-draped 22-year-old bride, I see a blissfully happy and painfully immature young girl – and I was a girl. God I was childish. In our first weeks of marriage, I was a ball of excitement. I remember hoping I would wake up in the middle of the night so I could remember I had a husband sleeping next to me. And that husband was Chris O'Loughlin. The guy I'd spent so much time dreaming of. I'd practised signing my name as Mrs O'Loughlin so many times, my hand was stained with blue ink. Chris had once told me I reminded him of his mum, Geraldine, and I desperately wanted to fill that void for him by loving him, laughing together and dancing when I did the ironing. Years later, Chris's aunt, his mother's sister, told me about a reoccurring dream their mother used to have. In it, she would open a door while cleaning the house, only to find three or four secret rooms she'd never seen before. I kid you not, I had the same reoccurring dream, night after night. Of course, it was the standard dream of a busy mum but, to me, it felt like a self-fulfilling prophecy. I had wanted to emulate Geraldine and my dream had come true, quite literally.

Chris was such a clean, can-do man, and incredibly generous with everyone who found themselves sitting at our table. He was always up by 6 am and would run up to 10 kilometres a day. The thought of Chris O'Loughlin lounging around in bed was unimaginable. We were opposites in that regard, I would think as I waved him off from the couch.

Looking back with a wiser mind and a pair of $20 reading glasses from the chemist, I can see that Chris and

I were probably doomed from the start. When I moved to Alice Springs as a newlywed, it felt like I had a new boss. I realise now I didn't know how to give voice to what I wanted. My mum was my boss growing up. I behaved myself then and now it felt like I had to behave a certain way again. Subliminally, perhaps I attracted exactly what I was trying to escape from at home. I felt like a child again. Rather than assert myself, I gave over the power. In my mind Chris was the joy killer, often cross at me for something, usually to do with spending money, buying flowers for the kitchen table, wanting to renovate the bathroom, or ringing up the phone bill calling my mum and sister Cate. Interstate phone calls were eye-wateringly expensive back then, but I was bored and lonely. I remember Chris coming home from work one afternoon with a face like thunder. He said, 'We got the phone bill today,' and didn't speak to me for the rest of the night. The next morning, he unplugged the phone and went off to work with it tucked under his arm. His parting shot was, 'Why can't you just write letters like the pioneer women would have done?'

The silence interrupted by yelling made my stomach turn. I'd had enough of that in my childhood. If you'll allow my melodrama, I felt like I was drowning.

When I found out I was pregnant with Henry six weeks after getting married, I was euphoric. Get married, have a baby – that was the natural order of a Catholic wife's life, and I was following the book to the letter. I had always loved babies and knew I wanted to be a mother. One of my happiest childhood memories was a surprisingly warm morning in autumn when I was fourteen. I woke up early to read my book in a cosy bed, revelling in the Indian summer drifting through my window. I kept waiting for someone to get up and tell me to stop reading and start getting ready for school, but the house was unusually still. I suddenly remembered daylight savings had ended, and I had another whole hour to myself. I snuck out of bed to make baby Emily her bottle and brought her to lie with me as I read. That was my definition of bliss.

After the doctor told me the happy baby news, I rang Chris from a phone booth in the Todd Mall, the pavement underfoot steamy in the midday heat. That phone call was the start of my heartbreak. He said, 'It's too soon, we're not financially ready.' It seemed to me this was his first reaction with every pregnancy. Every time I held a positive test in my hand, the excitement was overshone by the fear of the reprimand to come.

Nothing could outshine the birth of Henry, though. Chris's lack of early enthusiasm was eclipsed by the immense triangle of love I felt when I was in labour. The birth was awful; that's why it's called labour, it's a hard day's work. Henry was a brow presentation, his face was tilted the wrong way, so I had to have an emergency C-section, otherwise they said it would have taken me four days to have him. When I held Henry for the first time, I knew we were made for each other. He was so familiar and looked like a wise old man straight out of the womb. I felt innately confident as his mum and never questioned my ability as a mother.

Henry's birth day was easily the most romantic day of my life. Knowing Chris was the one other human on Earth to love this baby as much as I did, was an incredible connection. After thirty-four years, I can still remember what Chris was wearing and how he smelled: a blue checked flannelette shirt, with the lingering scent of fresh laundry straight out of the dryer. It was the most magical experience, and I want to tell girls to look forward to it and to savour it. Because then life gets boring and we all turn into arseholes again.

After Henry's baptism, we hosted lunch at our house for our family and friends. We drank red wine and toasted the beautiful baby. I was in my element: entertaining guests and doting over my precious son. I was holding Henry in my arms when a man came up to me and put his face so close to mine I could smell the alcohol on his breath and see the blood vessels in his cheek blushing with inebriety. He whispered into my ear, quiet enough so no one else would hear but loud enough to send a shiver down my spine, 'Thanks for today – and if you ever do anything to hurt this kid, I'll fucking kill you.'

I stepped back in shock. I think I may have even laughed, not knowing how to react to the verbal assault. I felt the same silencing fear as when the man, who was more than double my age, forced his tongue into my pubescent mouth in my childhood bathroom. What he said was so vulgar and violent, he knew I wouldn't repeat it. I should have raised my voice and said, 'What did you just say to me?' But I didn't. I cowered away from him, rocking my baby to sleep. Sometimes words are safer left unspoken.

The man's whispered threat underscored how separated I was from my own family and support network. I didn't have the words to call him out for his ugly and unwarranted comment, but I also felt like I didn't have anyone I could talk to about what had happened. I was incredibly lonely in the first few years of my marriage. I missed my brothers and sisters immensely, hence the phone bill. And I was sick of having the same argument with Chris. We started building resentments early on; I felt alone and overwhelmed with the load of parenting that weighed solely on my shoulders, and he begrudged having to carry all the financial burden on his shoulders. I think we both felt as trapped as each other. Our shoulders ached under the strain of our respective pressures. Chris was working twelve-hour days, waking up at 5 am and not getting home until after 7 pm, only stopping for a half-hour lunch break during which he ate a ham-and-cheese sandwich. As a small-business owner, he worked most weekends and often went back to the lab for a couple of hours after dinner, trying to get ahead, trying to shore up our future, trying to get away from me (I thought). I begged him to take a day off, just one day, to spend with me. He never did. I sulked on the couch, alone and forlorn.

When I was pregnant with my second child, Biddy, I left Chris. He was playing cricket and I left a scribbled note on the kitchen bench and boarded a flight to Adelaide with Henry. It was all very dramatic. I went and stayed with my parents, who didn't say a word about why I was there. Predictable silence.

After a couple of weeks, when I felt like I'd made my point, I flew back to Alice Springs. I didn't have any other option; I had a child and another one on the way, no job and nowhere to go. I had made my bed and it was time to go back and lie in it. Chris and I didn't speak while I was in South Australia. He didn't reach out to me or beg me to come home; but when I did, things slipped back to normal. He didn't say anything about my sudden departure or eventual return at the time but I felt like he would throw it back in my face during arguments for years to come. When Biddy was born, we lifted the needle from our well-worn record of arguments; it was a pause rather than a complete stop. The needle hovered above the vinyl.

My eldest sister, Genevieve, was coincidentally living in Alice at the time and spent a night at our place just after Biddy was born. We were sleeping in the same room, and under the blanket of darkness she said to me, 'When did you know?' She was asking me when I knew my marriage had been a mistake. I don't know if I answered her. But I was so touched that she asked the question in the darkness. We never spoke of it again.

*

Don't get me wrong, as the years passed I could give as good as I got. I was sharp with my tongue and brutal with my wit. When I went off, I really went off. I'd spit hurtful venom straight into Chris's eyes. Once he spat back, 'You've got a bloody mouth on you.' I returned the serve, 'Well, you've got the cheque book, the job and everything else. I've got to have *something*.'

I remember a fight that went too far and culminated in Chris slapping me. I'd been goading him to do it, willing him, pushing him. I wanted the trophy of him crossing the line, and the prize was a red mark across my left cheek. It was physical proof of how he made me feel. To Chris, the slap was earth shattering. He was devastated. He ran outside and climbed the hill at the back of our house in the middle of a thunderstorm, sitting in the rain for hours. When he finally came back inside soaking wet, the fight continued. 'We have nothing in common,' he yelled, for the thousandth or more time. 'I've been sitting on that hill praying for lightning to strike me dead.'

'Well, you see, we do have something in common then,' I barked back.

Poor Chris. What he didn't realise was that he'd already hurt me worse than that. I remember the moment that my heart slammed shut. It was Christmas time and I'd done all the shopping (as I did every year) and we packed the kids up for our annual pilgrimage to South Australia. Holidays without your own base is hard work. Moving from relative to relative with five kids in tow isn't a holiday at all; it's a mission. On this particular night in Adelaide, Bert had a raging ear infection and was screaming in the back seat. It was raining heavily and getting late and we hadn't yet secured a bed (or five) for the night. 'Can't we just please stay in a cheap hotel or a caravan park?' I begged, at the intersection of Cross Road and Goodwood Road, near the Big W where Jasmin had admonished the bullying mother all those years earlier. The torrent of words Chris yelled at me was prolonged. We were both tired and over it but there's nothing more humiliating than being yelled at in a car with your kids in the back seat. I stared out the window in silence and longed for the shouting to stop. In that moment I think I hated Chris. Something hardened in me that night at the intersection and it stayed hard for the rest of our marriage.

*

I remember staying with my sister Cate and her husband, Phil, one summer holidays when the kids were little. They had this beautiful house on The Parade in Norwood, Adelaide's chicest street, lined with fashion boutiques, bookstores and

Italian delis. We were crashing with them because we couldn't afford a hotel or a real holiday. I wasn't jealous of their newly renovated kitchen or their 1000-thread-count sheets – it was their closeness I envied. I cried into my pillow at night listening to Cate and Phil laughing in bed together, talking about the day that was, cuddled up in their fancy sheets. Oh, how I wished for a husband to laugh with.

Being married at a young age is tough wherever you are, but after I'd had my third baby – Tess – at age twenty-six, I truly felt the walls closing in on me in Alice Springs. It was a seriously male-dominated environment – oppressive and dusty in every sense of the word. The Northern Territory in the 1980s was akin to the rest of Australia in the 1960s and women had a pretty defined role. I was home alone with the kids every day doing all the parenting and heavy lifting. We were housewives who supported our blokes while they carved a living mostly out of small businesses or government positions. There was much backslapping at Friday arvo drinks. Every Friday arvo. But only for the blokes. There was no applause for the women raising children singlehandedly.

Still, it wasn't the parenting I resented; it was the lack of emotional support. Chris was a tactile dad; he bathed and changed the kids as much as me when he was at home, but he wasn't home very much at all. He didn't have enough hours in the day. All of the daily parenting decisions were left up to me, along with the Christmas shopping, doctor appointment bookings, birthday party planning and the rest of the emotional and mental load.

Even so, I loved being a mum. Having toddlers allowed me to turn life on its head and let the fun begin. I hated customs and rules when I was growing up. Why can't people eat cereal for lunch? Why three meals a day? Who would choose to have braised chops and vegetables for dinner when you could eat a pasty instead? Pasties are full of vegetables, I pondered. In my mind, the world was strewn with red tape and the fun police were on every corner. So, when I had kids of my own, fun became my middle name. I think I enjoyed myself as much as Henry, Biddy and Tess.

I would speak to them in varying accents most of the time, and our favourite game was me knocking on the door asking for a place to live.

'Hello, my name is Fiona and I'm looking for a house to live in,' I'd enquire. They would invite me inside and excitedly answer my list of real-estate questions.

'If I got tired at night-time, do you have anything I could sleep on?'

'Yes, yes, YES!!!' They would squeal with delight and grab my hands to drag me to my bedroom as though they'd solved an insurmountable problem.

'What if I want to wash my whole body at the end of the day? Do you have anywhere I could do that?' They would drag me to the bathroom and show me the shower as if it were a miraculous invention. On it went, from the washing machine in the laundry to the air conditioner in the living room. What a thrill.

Being a stay-at-home mum, I also relished spending one-on-one time with each of my kids. When Henry and Biddy started school, I would surprise them by turning up at recess and signing them out for a medical appointment, only to head to the movies for an afternoon of popcorn and cartoons. Tess was at preschool and aged four when she waltzed into the kitchen one morning and asked, 'Mum, am I sick today?'

Later that night over dinner, Chris asked little Tess how her day was. 'It was great. Mum and I stayed in bed and just kissed each other all morning.'

Luckily, Chris just laughed and shook his head.

Another afternoon, I was standing in the kitchen when someone called out for help with their homework from the dining room. 'Mum, how do you spell spectacular?'

'T-F-G-H-S-R-M-N.'

'*Mum!* I started writing that and it's in biro too!'

Chris sighed with exasperation and asked, 'Why do you do that?'

'Because it makes me laugh, and if they don't question my spelling, well, then we already know not to set our expectations too high.'

My children were raised in an unconventional and uncensored home, but at least we had some laughs. Mostly because laughter has been my oxygen and defence against gloom since my beginning as a born optimist. If you don't laugh, you'll …

My saving grace during those early days in Alice Springs was Chris's best friend, Nick. He was originally from Adelaide, too, but had moved to the red centre and worked as a fire fighter. I used to call him Mr February because he was so attractive and muscly. He looked like Matt Damon, but better. Because he worked shifts, Nick would drop by for coffee at our place most days and I'd bitch about Chris. Nick knew exactly what he was like, so we would laugh at his eccentricities together. He got it. Chris bitched about me to him as well, but Nick was a cheery middleman. He saw it from both sides. It meant the world to me to have someone to talk to who understood. Nick asked me questions and he listened to my answers. Better yet, he cared about what I had to say. Nick was a warm place in an often chilly house. He was probably that for Chris, too.

*

In the early 1990s, I started writing my column for the *Centralian Advocate*. I wrote about myself, the daily life of a housewife in Alice Springs. It was oh-so-relatable and hit a nerve with my fellow 'desperate housewives'. It was an escape for me, and I hoped for them, too. A small break from the monotony of motherhood. A welcome distraction from cooking, cleaning and the endless chores in between mealtimes. It wasn't anything revolutionary or shocking, but it still started conversations around town.

I remember Chris coming home from the Memorial Club and relaying a chat he had had with a local lawyer sitting at the front bar. 'You ought to smack your missus in the mouth for what she writes in the paper,' the lawyer said, as though I didn't deserve to have a voice, to tell my stories, to exist outside the family home.

Nevertheless, she persisted. I think I was paid just $15 a week for my column, but it was my money and I opened a bank account all of my own. Before I had my own PIN to memorise,

I'd been living hand-to-mouth with Chris, having to ask him for money every time I went grocery shopping. I had no idea how much our mortgage repayments were or how much money we had because Chris looked after the finances. He had been raised by his father to provide for his family. When I opened my bank account, Chris started depositing $250 a week into a housekeeping fund. I didn't get a single raise in our twenty-seven years together. I'd make a joke about having the world's stingiest boss. Chris might have called it budgeting but I can't help thinking it was financial control. When I started doing stand-up comedy, I would often have to call my friend Jasmin to wire me money, which was quite an ordeal back then. Once again, I felt trapped and desperately pined for independence and financial security. Once again, my situation was a sign of the times. Back then, husbands controlled the money and wives stuck to the budgets they were given.

By 1994, I was sticking it even harder to the local lawyer, writing and recording a weekly piece for ABC Radio: a three-minute vignette of 'the world according to me'. I also had a regular gig singing at the local piano bar, until I was fired for falling off the stage. That night, I was playing to my usual crowd of four, singing from my book of *101 Hits for Buskers*, and one of the regulars kept buying me glasses of Drambuie every time I hit a high note. Well, I hit enough high notes to push me over the edge, literally.

When I was (firmly) standing on stage, I felt free. I was addicted to the applause, even though most of the time I felt like I didn't deserve it. Maybe if they just clapped harder, I would feel validated. Maybe if they just wolf-whistled louder, I could shake off my imposter syndrome. Maybe if I got a standing ovation, I could prove the bloody lawyer wrong.

In an attempt to scratch my itch, I co-wrote a stage show called *Remote Control* with my sister-in-law Genevieve, about a woman who had become so addicted to her television that she entirely lost her grasp on reality. Yes, it was semi-autobiographical, based on the many, *many* hours I'd spent sitting in front of the idiot box wishing my life were a sitcom. One night, we played the show to a full house of five hundred people, and I went to bed afterwards happier than a human can be. I think I smiled in my sleep.

After *Remote Control*, I applied for and received a $600 grant from the Northern Territory Arts Minister to study stand-up comedy in Melbourne, leaving three babies at home (thank god for babysitters and aunts) to travel interstate to listen to crude jokes and inhale everything and anything comedic on offer. I started my comedy apprenticeship then and there, doing a ten-minute set about trams, caesareans and clothes at the Star and Garter Hotel in South Melbourne after chain-smoking a packet of Benson & Hedges in the front bar, trying to ease my nerves with nicotine. It was an inexperienced, cobbled together, think-on-your-feet performance, but they laughed. Better than that, they didn't boo me off the stage. It felt like going to a casino, playing blackjack and winning. I was hooked.

Comedians cut their teeth by doing three-to-five-minute unpaid sets at comedy clubs. My local club just happened to be 2259 kilometres away in Melbourne. After my first trip there, I went back as often as I could to do try-out mic nights, pushing myself to hone my routine and carve out a space on stage for myself. My trips to Melbourne were an opportunity to lift my head above the drowning weight of being a mum in the Northern Territory. I made sure I took a deep breath and filled my lungs in the graffiti-painted city streets before I returned to the normalcy and never-ending washing at home.

My trek to Melbourne involved catching a McCafferty's bus south to Adelaide and across to Victoria, watching the red dirt change to coastal shrubbery and then urban sprawl out the window. It took me three days, but we couldn't afford a direct flight. I really couldn't have made it harder for myself. I was a mum, living in the middle of Australia, trying to break in to one of the most competitive and cut-throat industries. I remember years later doing a TV show called *The World Stands Up* with a slate of international comedians, hosted by New York comic Dom Irrera. When he introduced me, he said: 'This woman lives in Alice Springs, Australia, and the chances of her making it at this level of comedy are one in five billion.' The odds were stacked against me, but I was never any good at maths.

*

As the mid-1990s pushed on, I was busy with a growing career, a steady stream of gigs and tours. Chris started to help me produce my shows (which basically meant he outlaid the cost of my performances and venue hire with our money) and was genuinely supportive of my career. We had four kids at home then and all the laundry and dishes that come with that. Greedily, I wanted more. I knew I wasn't finished having kids and I yearned to sniff that newborn smell again. One night after I had put Bert to bed, Chris confided to me that he didn't think he could handle the responsibility of having any more children. I was heartbroken. We talked for hours that night and for a long time afterwards.

A few months later, I suggested we go to counselling. We had reached a stalemate and neither of us was willing to budge from our respective corners and meet in the middle. I guess there's no such thing as meeting in the middle when it comes to having kids; you can't have half a baby. The counselling was gruelling and painful, and only got more volatile as the weeks went on. I knew that as much as I wanted another baby, I never, ever wanted to buy a pregnancy test with my heart in my throat. It had to be what we both wanted. I was sure Chris would change his mind.

Then I found out I was pregnant. Once again, Chris harboured the worry and I harboured the guilt. Before I knew it, I was plunged into morning sickness, but the excitement from the other kids brought Chris and I to the same place, and, by the time Mary-Agnes was born in 1997, every O'Loughlin was chafing at the bit to get their hands on our new baby. I knew she would be my last baby, and I wanted to cherish her accordingly.

*

I take my hat off to that girl on the McCafferty's bus on that first long trip to Melbourne. Because of her, I became one of the country's most loved comedians in my thirties, accepting the unofficial title of 'Australia's funniest mother of five', and winning the Best Newcomer Award at the 2001 Melbourne International Comedy Festival. Because of her, I was able to perform gigs in New York, Montreal, Singapore, London, Toronto and Edinburgh, where I scored five-star reviews. Edinburgh is a stage like no other. They say it's the toughest gig a comic can do. English comedian Johnny Vegas once described it as 'the performing equivalent of self-harm'. Stepping on stage feels like walking into the middle of the Colosseum: the audience are the Romans hungry for Christian blood. They show no mercy with their heckling.

'You suck!'

'Get off!'

'Yer nowt funnay!'

The crowd shouted at a young Russell Brand in 2001. He shouted back. The noise from the audience was frightening and Russell retaliated to the jeers by throwing something at them and encouraging them to throw glasses. A bloke in the front row obeyed, hurling a glass back at him, narrowly missing his head.

'Fiona, they're a really ugly crowd. I'll try and shut them up before I bring you on,' the emcee Adam Hills told me as he pushed past me backstage. I was crouching on the stairs when Russell stomped off stage, followed by a wave of shattered glass.

'Ladies and gentlemen, our next act is all the way from Alice Springs, Australia. Please make her welcome ... Fiona O'Loughlin!'

I registered my name and my cue to walk on stage, but I couldn't move. A whopping piece of glass was stuck through my pants and imbedded in my thigh. I took a deep breath, yanked it out and walked triumphantly into the middle of the Colosseum. Comedy is not for the weak hearted – or the weak stomached. Because of the resilience of that girl on the McCafferty's bus, I was able to stand on comedy's holiest stage with blood pouring down my leg and sweat trickling down my back.

God knows, I would have had a stiff drink after that show. The performers' bars at festivals are in a sense still part of a comedian's working day.

'How was your show?'

'Shitful audience, so I pulled the parachute on my new stuff and went back to the old rope.'

'How was your show?'

'I had a heckler. He got thrown out at the twenty-minute mark, I should have gone with him.'

'How was your show?'

*

By the early 2000s, with five kids at home aged between three and fourteen, I was a regular at festivals around the world, selling out shows, winning awards and scoring TV appearances on shows such as *Midday* and *Hey Hey It's Saturday*, and later *Last Comic Standing*, *Rove*, *Good News Week* and *Spicks and Specks*. I would even go on to film a pilot episode for my own TV series called *Life at the Top* for Channel 7. We stopped fostering when my career really started to pick up, and I filled that hole in my heart with my peers.

I felt such a camaraderie with my fellow comedians. I was most at home sitting backstage at a festival or at the pub after a gig, debriefing, laughing and holding court. There is no small talk with comedians. Because we're so used to baring our soul on stage, we dive straight into the hard, messy, vulnerable stuff. Our friendships get deep fast. You could spend half an hour with another comic and walk away feeling like you've known them for years. The conversations are open, unjudged, frank and – as you'd expect – fucking hilarious. We were a rat pack of misfits and I truly felt like I belonged.

I remember sitting next to Canadian comic Mike Wilmot at the Peter Cook Bar during the Melbourne International

Comedy Festival one year. I'd only met him an hour earlier and I was instantly charmed by his wickedly dry sense of humour and razor-sharp repartee. A woman sat down next to us; we'd met before and I knew she was quite high up in the festival, but I couldn't for the life of me remember her name. Forgetful Fi was in fine form. I leaned over to Mike and whispered, 'Do you mind doing that thing where you introduce yourself so I can find out her name? I can't afford to forget it. She's a big deal.' He nodded. A couple of minutes later he reached over me and asked the woman bluntly, 'Hey, what's your name?'

'Michelle,' she offered, graciously.

'Her name's Michelle, you duplicitous bitch,' he dead-panned me. We erupted with laughter.

Like most comedians, my material was inspired by my life, the brutal (but mostly boring) reality of being a mother and wife. Like most comedians, I exaggerated my own persona for comic effect, playing up the shit-mum schtick. Like most comedians, I talked about the people in my life, telling jokes at my family's expense.

Chris would complain that he thought I was always setting him up to be the punchline of a joke. But in my opinion, he did it all by himself. He can be blunt and eccentric, and sometimes I had no choice but to laugh at his mannerisms. But mostly, I just laughed at myself and my own flaws. I would joke, 'I'm the laziest person I know. I don't do any housework between the hours of 9 am and 4 pm because I don't see the point if I don't have an audience.'

I can thank my kids for some of my best one-liners, like this ripper: 'People say to me, "Oh my God, Fiona, how do you juggle it: five kids and an international comedy career?" I don't. I leave them.'

And this: 'It's an awful lot of kids, isn't it, in this day and age, five kids, but we're committed. We're going to keep trying till we get one we like.'

They almost write themselves: 'I was in Sydney a while back doing a season at the Opera House and I got a terrible review in the *Sydney Morning Herald*. The critic said I was immature and mean to my kids. I immediately returned an email to her, which read, "They started it."'

Once I was recognised in a supermarket in Canada, and the adoring fan said, 'Ooh, you're that woman from Australia, the one that drinks too much and hates her kids.' For the record, I don't hate my kids. It's very hard to bitch about kids you actually adore. Henry, Biddy, Tess, Bert and Mary-Agnes all have an intimate knowledge of how stand-up works and I like to think they haven't taken my gags to heart. I used to say, 'My kids know what I'm like. I'm not particularly their favourite stand-up either.'

I tried to convince myself that my career did my children more good than harm, that I was setting a fantastic example for them, following my dreams, taking risks and making a living. What sort of mother would I be if I ignored my hankerings? A miserable one. Every time I left for a tour or a festival, I'd tell myself I wasn't leaving them forever. It was only a month and they were all safe. My mother played golf three days a week and I turned out *totally* fine.

Plus, being a comedian had its perks. Chris and I were invited to meet the Queen on her visit to Alice Springs in 2000. They tried to find fifty of the flashest people in Alice, and we scraped onto the list somehow – probably at number 49 and 50.

Inside the restaurant the Chief Minister of the Northern Territory gave us a pep talk: 'Her Majesty will be arriving any second. Please, no pushing or shoving. She will come to you all individually.' Wow, thank God he pointed that out. I resisted all my urges to push to the front and curtsy like an idiot. I was still drinking at the time and there was a free bar, so before I knew it, I'd had five glasses of sparkling wine and the Queen was leaving the event. There were only two people who hadn't met the Queen: Chris and me. I didn't really care, I was pissed. Across the room, I looked at Chris and knew exactly what he was thinking. He had the doe eyes of a little boy, and an expression that said, *The Queen is leaving, and I will never, ever get the chance to meet her again.* I just knew he was going to do something embarrassing, so I tried to get to them before he could. It was like one of those bad dreams where I was walking in slow motion, unable to stop the horror I could see happening. Before I got to Chris, he blocked the Queen's passage to leave. He stuck his hand out and said, 'G'day, I'm Chris,' breaching all the protocol. One does not offer their hand to the Queen; she has to offer hers to one first. To her credit, the Queen shook Chris's hand, albeit limply. I tried to remedy the situation and in a nervous panic I turned to the man standing next to me without looking at him and said too loudly, 'Did he just fuck up!?'

I kid you not, the Duke of Edinburgh leaned down and whispered in my ear, 'Not as much as you just did.'

On another occasion, Chris and I were invited to an art exhibition opening to rub shoulders with the red centre's cultural elite and a famous artist visiting from Sydney. I knew next to nothing about art; the only painter I was vaguely aware of was Allyson Parsons who is from the same stretch of the

Yorke Peninsula as me. After about six glasses of personality, I sidled up to the famous Sydney artist and put on my best posh, highbrow voice. 'Do you know Allyson Parsons' work?' I asked the famous artist, who shook his head. 'Oh, you should really check her work out, she's fantastic! She does such incredibly intricate landscape paintings, and she's blind.' Even as the words came out of my mouth, I knew something about the story wasn't quite right.

'She's blind?' the artist was shocked. Almost as shocked as me.

All of a sudden, the artist was very interested in what I had to say and about eight other people gathered around.

'She paints very fine detailed landscape pieces and she's blind?' he asked again.

'Well, I mean, um, I think she has some peripheral vision.' I tried to dig myself out of the conversational hole I was in.

Chris was silent the whole car trip home. Driving down our street, the air was frosty and awkward. When he parked in the driveway and turned off the ignition, he finally said, 'Deaf. Allyson Parsons is deaf.'

Years later, I told that joke at an Adelaide Fringe show at the Nova Theatre on Rundle Street. My manager grabbed me after the gig and told me a couple wanted to meet me. He escorted me to the balcony and introduced me to 'Mr and Mrs Parsons', Allyson's mum and dad. I nearly fainted. They loved the joke, though, and invited me to open Allyson's next exhibition re-telling the story of my humble brag gone wrong.

*

When my career really took off, I was away for up to six months a year. Poor Chris. It must have been truly awful for him. Well, actually, I know for a fact it was. I fully understand how lonely and isolating it is to care for kids on your own with an absentee spouse. Chris was a loving dad, but it's not a one-man or a one-woman job. His best friend, Nick, was always around to lend a hand and I would hire nannies from the backpacker hostel or fly my aunt over from Perth to look after the kids when I was away for extended periods. Still, Chris resented my absence, understandably. We had the same fight over and over again until the record was well and truly scratched.

'So, you travel the world and I just have to rot away in that dental lab?'

'Sell the damn dental lab and come with me.'

'I have to work!'

'So do I!'

The truth was, we were both right. Having five kids is bloody expensive and we were determined to send them to boarding school in Adelaide for the final two or three years of their education so they had the same opportunities as we did. We never had any money. Our family holidays were only ever packing the kids up in the car and driving to South Australia to stay with relatives. The narrative we were taught in our youth – that women should stay home and raise the kids – was financially impractical. Whether we wanted to or not, we both had to work, and my job just happened to involve travelling the world and cracking jokes.

When I wasn't on the road, I was on the couch. I was exhausted. After working hard on tour, I'd come home to work even harder. The place was always a bomb site when I arrived back, dirty plates and clothes everywhere, but at least the kids were always excited to see me. I know they missed me when I was away, but I don't believe they ever resented me for it, and they revelled in our time together.

Apart from smothering my kids in kisses, I became very anti-social in Alice Springs and spent most of my time watching TV. I think I invented binge-watching. My joy of joys was introducing my kids to *The Young Ones* when they were old enough to watch it with me. I was enthralled by the madness of it, the anarchy, the lunacy and the insane characters. Experiencing it again child by child was like reliving the magic all over. Rick (played by Rik Mayall) was my favourite character and most of the kids liked him best too. But I can still hear thirteen-year-old Henry's roar of laughter when Vyvyan, the metal-head medical student, didn't like the show he was watching and so kicked his booted foot straight through the TV screen. TV was an escape. The best part? I didn't have to leave the couch.

I was the life of the party on tour and at festivals, so at home I just wanted to be a loner. Being home was a chance for me to lick my wounds and recover from the mischief (and subsequent humiliation) of the big nights that turned into early mornings that turned into excruciating hangovers. In Alice, I avoided parties, get-togethers and alcohol in general (except for the unavoidable Friday night drinks at our dinner table). So when an American man living in Alice called Butch kept calling me and leaving messages about an improv troupe, I ignored him. I told you, I'm a lazy bitch. It wasn't until Chris ran into him down the street and told me I should ring him back that I dragged myself off the couch and made an effort. I went to meet Butch at the Totem Theatre, a corrugated-iron shed on the banks of the dry Todd River, one Saturday morning in 1999 with my usual hangover. My head thumped in the roaring heat. Butch worked in town and his wife had a job at the military base in Alice. They had a little girl the same age as Mary-Agnes. His pants were a bit high, but he was a one-time stand-up comic from Texas and was interested in setting up a local improv troupe, so I was all ears.

I'm not exaggerating when I say, I've never laughed as hard meeting someone as the first time I met Butch. He was breathtakingly funny – literally, I choked with laughter as tears ran down my cheeks. We became fast friends as we set up the improv group we named 'The Laughing Stock'. When he was working in town and I was at home, Butch would come over for lunch and we'd heckle Oprah together watching midday TV. Our troupe started putting on regular shows at Witchetty's theatre at the Araluen Arts Centre and we built a loyal following. It was truly a great time in my life, filled with belly laughs and in-jokes.

One night in the early 2000s, Butch knocked at my front door. Sadly, he told me he'd been offered a job in America and was moving home with his family. By that stage he was also working at the military base with his wife and they had applied to stay in Alice Springs, but their request was rejected.

We had grown incredibly close – Butch once told me I was his best friend – but nothing physical ever happened between us. My inner Catholic wouldn't let me entertain the sinful idea of cheating on Chris. I would never have acted on any feelings that I may have developed and Butch never knew.

When he left Alice Springs, I would drive past his house and weep. I grieved for the loss of our friendship, the banter, the Oprah trash talk. We stayed in touch over email, and when I saw his name pop up in my inbox, my heart would swell. Once, as I was walking out the door to catch a taxi to the airport for a corporate gig in Sydney, I opened my inbox to find a very sweet email from Butch. I'd been venting to him about Chris and he replied with calm, kind words, the exact words I needed to hear – I felt loved and valued. Even if it was purely platonic, I knew I had to delete the email, but I selfishly wanted to print off a copy so I could keep re-reading it. I pressed print as the taxi started beeping its horn. Like an episode of *Seinfeld*, the printer jammed; I kept pressing print and the taxi kept beeping. I raced out the door like Kramer in a kerfuffle.

Later that week, we were watching *Blue Heelers* on the couch when Tess complained she couldn't print off a school project, something was wrong with the printer. Chris jumped up to fix it – Mr Can Do – and out spat twenty-five copies of Butch's email, which Chris construed as a love letter rather than what it was, a note to cheer up a sad friend. 'What's all this, then?' he asked, waving the paper in my face.

'Weird, hey. I think Butch must have had a few when he wrote it,' I brushed it off.

Chris had Googled 'emotional affairs' and became obsessed with the idea that I had been unfaithful. But I refused to go down for it because nothing physical happened between Butch and me, and as far as I was concerned, I hadn't crossed any lines. Chris and I went to couples counselling and at the second session, Chris asked that I cut all contact with Butch. So, I did.

In hindsight, that's when we should have ended our marriage. For both our sakes. Every time we fought, we pulled at old wounds and often Chris would put a discussion of divorce on the table. I think he felt as trapped as I had in the early years of our marriage. My drinking was starting to get more and more out of control, and deep down in a place I was reluctant to visit in my soul, I knew I was in trouble. Hindsight's a real bitch.

CHAPTER 2

AM I AN ALCOHOLIC?

A S MY CAREER STARTED TO ESCALATE, SO TOO DID MY drinking. If I had a good show, I'd drink to celebrate. If I had a bad show, I'd drink to drown my sorrows. Comedy allowed me to hide my addiction in plain sight, using my alcoholism as material for comedy and using comedy as an excuse for my alcoholism. Of all the camouflages a problem drinker can have, the world of stand-up has got to be one of the most convincing.

I clearly remember my point of no return. It was the day after my brother-in-law Justin's fortieth birthday party at his house in Alice Springs. I was horrendously hungover. My head was pounding, and my stomach was churning like a bile washing machine stuck on spin cycle. I was hosting the recovery lunch at our place, catering for twenty people, with crap and kids everywhere. My kids were aged between three and fourteen then. One of my friends noticed how green I looked and pulled me into the kitchen. She poured me a shot of whisky and said, 'Down that and you'll feel better.' And I did, and I did. It was a pivotal moment in my life – I'd found a solution to getting through a hangover: and that solution was to keep drinking. Hair of the dog was the beginning of the end.

That moment was more dangerous for me than the first time I got drunk as an eighteen-year-old. I was getting ready to go to the Highway Inn disco with my girlfriend Liza and downed a Vegemite jar full of Bacardi Rum while she was in the shower. I'd never been drunk before and wanted to know what it felt like. How did it feel, Fiona? I felt like I was ten-foot tall, funnier and warmer. And apparently, I was! Well, not ten-foot tall, but funnier and warmer.

Liza and I were to join our other school friends that night, to prowl the streets of Adelaide, looking for boys. There were only two types of boys to choose from back then, Sacred Heart and Rostrevor boys. These were the two major Catholic boys' colleges at the time, and I never once entertained the thought of marrying outside of that pool. We hung out with a gang of boys including Pat Tohl and Simon Fosdike. My sister Cate spent hours pining over Pat Tohl. I thought she was bonkers for caring so much. I didn't understand how a boy could rip your heart out, I was far too busy kissing them, partying with them and flirting with them; I gave no thought to getting attached to them. I was mad for Simon Fosdike and I still have delicious memories of pashing him all night with Queen's 'We Are the Champions' playing in the background. Any night I got to pash Simon Fosdike was a good night.

I remember doing a fundraising gig in Adelaide fifteen years ago for Sacred Heart and seeing their wrinkled faces in the crowd. The boys I'd grown up with – and lusted over – were now middle-aged men, with beer guts, receding hairlines and frown lines. I jumped gleefully on stage and laughed through the microphone, 'Well, you want me now, don't you?'

As much as we were sent to Cabra College for an education, the ultimate goal, I guess, was for us to meet and mingle with and eventually marry other South Australian Catholics. In around 1980, Cate asked the question of Mum at the Warooka kitchen table: 'So, are you saying we *have* to marry Catholics?' She had started going out with a Protestant pig farmer about

65 kilometres away and it wasn't sitting well with Mum or anyone else, at the time. Mum responded with, 'Well, no, but what I'm saying is that it would just be easier if you did.' Asked and most definitely answered.

I never drank alcohol for the taste, just the feeling, the invincibility, the crutch. Given the choice, I'd always pick spirits and sweet cruisers over wine. When I once ordered a Kahlua and Coke at the front bar of the Warooka Hotel standing next to my dad, the carpet sticky underneath our feet, he looked at me and said, 'You'd want to be very careful with that stuff.' I've never forgotten the warning but didn't manage to heed it. Sorry, Dad. There is alcoholism on both sides of my family, and my sister Cate has always said we were all sitting ducks. One of us was bound to end up an alcoholic. I drew the short straw (and sucked on it until the glass was empty).

I justified my binge-drinking by telling myself beer was better than drugs. I didn't like marijuana, the popular drug of choice back then, very much. On the few occasions I'd had a puff on a joint, it made me retreat into my mind and think too much. I wanted an escape from my thoughts, not a magnifying glass for them. I remember going to my cousin's wedding in the Adelaide Hills. It was such a beautiful ceremony and the reception was held at a homestead under a marquee on the lawn surrounded by rolling hills of acreage. We crowded under the marquee for the speeches. It was standing room only and we all squeezed in trying to hear the declarations of love and embarrassing stories. My brother Justin was standing in front of me, trapped between people, unable to scream or run away without drawing unwanted attention to himself. Naturally, I thought it was the perfect opportunity to give him a mighty wedgie. *Got you now*, I said in my head, shoving my hand down the back of his trousers. As his underwear cut deep into his groin, he turned around and … it wasn't Justin.

I ran for the hills, literally. I was breathless by the time I sat down next to a bloke I'd grown up with but wasn't especially close to. I told him what I'd done, and he passed me a joint. I puffed on it so hard I choked. My coughing fit turned to severe anxiety. I was sure everyone was judging me and laughing at me. Sitting on the hill, I was paralysed with paranoia and turned the same shade of green as the grass beneath me. A man came and sat down beside me and tried to strike up a conversation. His words sounded like gobbledygook and his voice hung in the air like clouds, changing shape before floating away into oblivion. I tried to catch them, but I couldn't move. I turned to the man and said, 'I'm so sorry, I'm really stoned and can't understand you.' Except he wasn't a man, but a tall child, who ran back to his mum in confusion and fear, telling her about the crazy lady sitting on the hill smoking drugs. I also wanted to run into my mum's arms, but I couldn't move. Family breakfast the next morning was excruciating.

As well as telling myself alcohol was the lesser evil of drugs, I also justified my drinking problem by saying, 'I don't drink every day, so it's not that bad.' I could go three weeks without drinking, but when I did drink, I would drink and drink and drink. At social events, I still felt a responsibility to make everyone happy, to fill the silence, to be the life of the party. After a particularly big Friday night around our dining table, Chris chastised me for embarrassing myself, talking too much and apparently telling one of my best friends her baby looked like Laurie Oakes. I snapped back, 'Well, maybe if someone else was prepared to say something funny, I wouldn't have to drink a bottle of vodka every Friday night.'

In my mind, my humour was directly linked to vodka. Downing two mini-bar bottles of Smirnoff became my pre-show ritual, my rabbit-foot talisman, my trusty crutch. Two 50mL bottles equalled three standard drinks, which just so happened to be the exact amount I needed to be funny but not sloppy. It was an art, a science, a mathematical equation

I perfected over the years. The thought of walking on stage sober was an unpassable notion. If I went on stage without three standard drinks in me, I would bomb. Worse than that, everyone would realise what a fraud I was. The game would be up. I truly believed that I needed Dutch courage to perform, as much as I believed the world was round and hell was like a baby screaming for the mother it never had. That was my truth.

*

It didn't feel like a slap in the face. It felt like a grubby, unwanted hand rubbing my thigh at the end of the night when my speech was too slurred to shout *stop* or whisper *please don't*. It didn't taste like a bitter pill. It tasted like morning mouthwash trying to mask yesterday's vodka. It didn't hit me all of a sudden. I knew it was coming. It hit me over and over again like waves of nausea rising in my stomach. The realisation that I was an alcoholic was an overdue jolt. I saw it coming, but I closed my eyes tight, keeping it blurry in the distance.

The first time I said it out loud was in 2000. 'I think I'm an alcoholic,' I whispered to Chris and my sister Emily, who is also a comedian and an actress. We were staying in a Melbourne hostel while Emily and I performed 'Fiona and Her Sister (and Some Guy)', which Chris was producing.

'There's something wrong with me. When I drink, I can't stop,' I admitted. It was scary saying the words out loud, but scarier to keep them bottled up inside. Sometimes words are safer spoken.

Chris's reaction to my admission was kind and convincing. He told me I was not an alcoholic. 'Besides, you don't drink vodka for breakfast.' Maybe I didn't then, but that's exactly where I ended up ...

At the time, I felt like I didn't have a right to be anything, so if Chris said I wasn't an alcoholic, then I wasn't an alcoholic. But deep down, I knew. I had a problem, and I didn't know how to fix it. For once, I couldn't fill the silence or ease the tension by being the life of the party. Being the life of the party was the problem.

I recall gagging in the physical agony of a hangover on a tour while attempting to brush my teeth one morning in a hotel room in Launceston. I stared right through my reflection in the mirror and spoke out loud to the hateful witch that was myself staring back at me, 'You are so sick. You are so sick.'

It was a mantra I was to repeat many more times over many more hangovers. As usual, hell turned to hilarity and gave me another excuse to keep drinking. Hangovers make great material. That morning in Launceston a few hours after my chat in the mirror, I sat around a table in a cafe with a handful of other comedians. We ordered greasy breakfasts to soak up the booze and whinged about our splitting headaches. Tom Gleeson wondered out loud what could be the worst possible scenario a person could find themselves in, in a hungover state. Greg Fleet jumped in first, and then everyone piled on top.

'Going hiking with your dad.'

'Helping your grandma move into a nursing home.'

'Helping your grandma move into a nursing home in Karratha.'

'Going to a dry Jehovah's Witness wedding in Broken Hill.'

'Being a Jehovah's Witness in Broken Hill and going door-knocking in 40-degree heat.'

My phone started ringing and I stepped outside to talk to Chris. Half an hour later, I returned to the table as everyone was finishing their breakfast. 'I've just found out what's the worst possible thing someone can be put through during a hangover.'

'What?'

'Having your husband call you from Alice Springs and read out loud every word of five kids' report cards.' Laughs all round.

*

My annual pilgrimage to the Melbourne International Comedy Festival was a month of excess, debauchery and lawlessness. For those four glorious weeks, comedians ruled the streets and ran wild. After our shows, we'd head to the Peter Cook Bar at Melbourne Town Hall until midnight and then on to the Hi-Fi Bar until sun-up. We'd spill drinks and smoke inside, even though the latter was illegal. I nearly coughed up a lung laughing one night at the Peter Cook Bar when my friend and English comedian John Moloney articulated the absurdity of our profession to a knowing crowd. He picked up an imaginary phone and started to talk to an imaginary person from a job agency on the other end.

'Yes, hello. Um, I would like a job, please … Yes, I'm prepared to work between twenty-four and forty minutes a day. I'd prefer evenings, of course, as I need to sleep most of the day. I will need to swear quite a lot while I'm working. Obviously, I'll choose my own uniform and quite often I'll be drunk. And if I should begin not to enjoy myself during work, I will need to reserve the right to tell everyone to go fuck themselves and leave my job early. Obviously in such instances, I should still like to be paid and retain the right to turn up to my work or not the next day, depending on my mood.'

Another night, looking across the smoky bar before last call, I remember seeing a comedian light up a joint in the middle of the room. No one batted an eyelid, except to say, pass that over here. I'd only ever touched dope and alcohol, so when another comic gave me an ecstasy tablet, I put it in my make-up case and promptly forgot all about it.

A few years later, I vividly recall sitting in the gutter outside the Hi-Fi with comedian Sarah Kendall at 5 am waiting for our taxis. It had been a huge night. We would have been quite the vision: messy hair, smeared lipstick, shoes off. She was psyching herself up to face her mother at home, who would hug her tightly when she walked through the door and say, 'You smell like O'Loughlin. She's a bad influence on you, Sarah. You're not as strong as her.'

When I returned to my hotel room, I had to pack my bags and head to the airport to catch a flight home to the wrath of the man I now thought of as Constable Chris (not a good way to keep a marriage). I felt like death. The thought of my impending hangover (which I guessed would hit me like a tsunami at 3 pm) and the look on Chris's face when he saw the state of me, made me gag. I washed my face and reapplied my make-up, trying to hide my drunkenness with foundation and a nice lippie. I blurred my eyes when I looked in the mirror because I couldn't stand the sight of myself. As I searched for my mascara wand in my make-up case, I opened a zip and found the three-year-old ecstasy tablet. It had been there all this time and I'd unwittingly flown across the world with it in my carry-on luggage. Later, on stage, I would joke, 'I could have been Schapelle's roomie.'

I was drunk at 6 am in my forties, so I thought, *Why not?* It seemed like a good enough morning as any to try my first Class-A drug. The love I felt for the steward and my fellow passengers on my three-hour flight from Melbourne to Alice was deep and abiding. The eccy ripped through me and lasted all day. Chris didn't know what was going on when I landed. He had expected to pick up grumpy guts with a raging hangover, but I was so deliriously happy and thrilled to see my family. Later that day, Tess said, 'I like you like this.'

*

Comedy is a bipolar industry. The highs are dizzying, and the lows make your stomach drop like the Big Dipper ride at Luna Park. One of the lowest moments in my career came towards the end of 2004. Months earlier, I'd filmed the pilot for my sitcom *Life at the Top*, about a married couple, Fiona and Scott, who had made some questionable financial decisions and found themselves relocating to Darwin from Sydney with their only son in an attempt to restore their bank balance – and sanity. Naturally, hilarity ensued for Fiona (played by me) and Scott (played by William McInnes from my favourite show *Blue Heelers*). The script was pure gold, the filming in Darwin was seamless and the viewing party we had with the crew was a roaring success. I waited with anticipation for a phone call from one of the suits at Channel 7 giving us the green light for a full season. They'd told me I'd hear before the end of the year, and I knew that 80 per cent of pilots made went on to be commissioned. Even though maths was never my strong suit, I knew the odds were in my favour this time.

By mid-December, I started to feel anxious about the silent phone, and by the time we packed the car and headed to the Yorke Peninsula for Christmas I was feeling devastated. Deep down, I knew that *Life at the Top* had been passed on. I'd read in *The Age* that Channel 7 had bought a new program from America called *Desperate Housewives* and commissioned reality show *Dancing with the Stars*. There was no mention of a local sitcom based in the Northern Territory.

We held Christmas at my brother Richard's house, Cletta, the original homestead that my great-grandfather had built just outside of Warooka. All of the Tahenys were there and it should have been a magical time. I tried to fill the 'life of the party' role that I'd been playing since I was a kid, but my heart wasn't in it. I was so sad. By the time the new year started, I knew *Life at the Top* was over. I cried myself stupid in nearly every room of the farmhouse. It seemed self-indulgent at first to be so heartbroken over an intangible project, but nonetheless, I grieved.

I woke up crying and fell asleep crying for a good ten days. It actually felt like someone had killed my family (albeit my fictional one). Channel 7 had taken Fiona out to the parking lot and shot her in the head in cold blood. I mourned the loss of a dream that had been more than fifteen years in the making. I had been bitten by the black dog of depression and I knew from experience the only way through it was to feel it and wait for it to let go.

My son Henry once explained to me what you should do if you ever get caught in a rip at the beach. 'You just let it take you, Mum. Don't fight it and go with it along the shoreline until it eventually lets go.'

I think the same advice should apply to anyone caught in a severe rip of melancholy. Take the time to go with it and for

God's sake, don't try to fight it on your own. Fighting it is how most people drown.

After a couple of solitary weeks wandering around Cletta in a nervous breakdown of sorts, I felt the old house wrap its arms around me and start nursing me back to life, strangely enough by allowing me to trawl through the past.

It's an incredible thing to lie on a bed and stare at the same ceiling that your great-grandmother must have pondered a hundred years earlier. I didn't know much about Margaret Sweeny, but I found myself wondering about my great-grandmother and what her life must have been like. What did she make of this windy, stubbled place? When did she see her first brown snake? Did she scream blue murder? Where did she have her nine babies? Did she scream blue murder? Who did she turn to when she had her first fight with her husband Francis Taheney? Did she scream blue murder?

I posed all these questions to Margaret's portrait in the dining room, but she didn't answer me.

*

With my sitcom dreams crushed, I went back to doing what I did best: performing and drinking. I was booked to do a show at the Adelaide Fringe and planned a girls' weekend with Biddy, then seventeen, and Tess, fifteen, who were at boarding school down there. I cried each time a kid packed their suitcase for boarding school but soothed myself with happy memories from my own high school years in Adelaide. I knew deep down boarding school was the right place for them to be as teenagers, if only to teach them how to catch a tram and wear shoes. When I visited the girls, I booked a nice hotel and promised to take them formal-dress shopping in the morning before my show. It didn't happen. I got filthy drunk the night before and couldn't move. I spent the whole day in bed, trying to muster enough energy for my gig at the Rhino Room that night. This is the selfish side of alcoholism; it makes you put vodka before your children. It makes you break promises. It makes you hurt the ones you love the most. By this stage, I knew my kids worried about my drinking and crossed their fingers at parties with me, hoping I wouldn't go overboard and embarrass us all. They had all seen me tipsy after gigs before – over the years I took each of them to different festivals from Montreal to Melbourne, and Edinburgh to the east coast of Queensland – but this was a new low.

I knew I'd royally screwed up. I could see the heartbreak and disappointment on the girls' faces when I finally crawled out of bed. I called my friend Christine from Adelaide and she sat with us in the green room before the show, acting as a mediator and comforting Biddy and Tess. As the emcee cracked jokes on stage and the audience laughed along, Christine said, 'The girls want you to know how disappointed they are.' I shared that. I was so sick of myself and my broken-record-drinking bullshit. All I wanted to do was to cuddle my girls and make it up to them, but I could hear the emcee wrapping up his act and I knew I had to step on stage and perform my shit-mum schtick with two upset children sitting backstage.

'Do you have anything you want to say to the girls, Fiona?' Christine asked, as I looked sideways at the stage.

'Yes, um … Would either of you like my autograph?' I dead-panned. They both cracked a brief smile. Like I said, I did what I do best: joked the pain away. If you don't laugh, you'll cry, and I couldn't ruin my mascara before I went on stage.

The next morning, I dropped the girls back to boarding school in a taxi before heading to the airport to go home to Alice. I'll never forget the sight of Tess, staring out the window blinking away tears as we drove through the streets of Adelaide. I was so caught up in my own hell, I didn't know Tess was being bullied at school and Biddy was developing an eating disorder. They were teenage girls and they needed their mum.

With tears rolling down her cheek, I could feel Tessy wishing for what she didn't have. Praying for a different mother, a better mother, a sober mother. It's what they both deserved.

Biddy bought her own formal dress for her Year 12 graduation. It was a striking pink vintage number. She looked beautiful.

*

Even though drinking was part of the job description for a comedian, I've never blamed my profession for causing my alcoholism. There has been a long-held misconception that my 'carnival family' had led me astray, but the opposite was true. My 'eclectic' family of fellow comedians looked out for me and never judged me. They didn't encourage me to party or interfere with my sobriety. I did that all on my own.

In 2006, I had the honour of being the only international guest on a road trip through Canada with the Montreal 'Just for Laughs' comedy festival. I only knew one of the comedians at the start of that tour, an LA-based comic called Alonzo Boden, but, having an innate trust in any fellow joke-meister, I quietly filled in my five tour buddies on my struggle with the bottle. Touchingly, they were all understanding and supportive of the Aussie alcoholic they'd just met. Barring one night off in Toronto and another night to celebrate the tour, I was blessedly able to experience touring across the most beautiful country in the world without my nasty hangover companion.

I have one standout memory from that joyful tour. I was having breakfast in a hotel in Saint John in New Brunswick on the first morning. The hotel dining room looked out to the ocean. A huge fishing trawler was docked so close that I could watch three or four fishermen beginning their day, and God bless one of them who actually smoked a pipe and had a beard to complement the scene. I really did pinch myself as I tucked into a Mexican frittata with the excitement ahead of at least twenty Canadian cities to see. Then, like an old friend tapping me on the shoulder, I noticed the music that was playing in the restaurant. Bloody joy! Playing softly in the background was my favourite song 'From St Kilda to Kings Cross' by Paul Kelly, who sang about spending thirteen hours on a bus, pressing his face against the window and watching the white lines on the road rush past. It was the perfect soundtrack to a perfect moment in time. If only all my tours were as blissful and well scored as that one.

A couple of years later I found myself sitting across the table from Paul Kelly having an early dinner in Scotland before our respective shows at the Edinburgh Festival Fringe. I was fat-tongued all night. I could barely speak a word without blushing or stumbling over my sentences. At the time, we were both working on our first memoirs and Paul asked me if my book was going to be all stand-up jokes. I told him it would be a standard memoir with humour weaved through naturally. Then I said the most outrageous thing to Paul Kelly, Australia's best storyteller and songwriter. 'You know, there's a real rhythm to words ...' I nearly choked as I finished the sentence.

*

By 2008, I was in the thick of addiction. In between comedy festivals, I was admitted to hospital several times for alcohol poisoning; or in between hospital admissions, I attended comedy festivals. Whichever way you look at it, I was juggling my disease with my work and dropping balls all over the place. On the last night of the Melbourne International Comedy Festival in March, Rod Quantock and Fiona Scott-Norman hosted a variety show interviewing Lawrence Mooney under the bright lights of the Spiegeltent. Lawrence was off his chops on God knows what and was highly entertaining. Rod asked him, 'Where does Fiona O'Loughlin fit into the Melbourne comedy scene?' And Lawrence answered, 'Oh, she's Dorothy Parker,' comparing me to the infamous American poet who wrote some of the wisest cracks ever written, including this ripper, 'You can lead a horticulture, but you can't make her think.'

Lawrence's answer was such an extraordinary statement. I remember walking down St Kilda Road to catch the number 72 tram home and it hit me that I was numb to so much in my life. The good and the bad. If only I could feel that compliment. If only I could see myself the way Lawrence did. In that moment, I decided I wanted to beat my addiction, because I wanted to feel these big, beautiful moments. I wanted to prove I wasn't a fraud. I wanted to *be* the Dorothy Parker of the Melbourne comedy scene – not one of her brutal quips, 'Take me or leave me; or, as is the usual order of things, both.'

CHAPTER 3

THE INCIDENT

W HEN I WOKE UP IN A HOSPITAL BED, MY FIRST
thought was, *I don't remember buying a nightie that
does up at the back.* My second thought was, *Oh fuck.* Piecing
together flashes of memory from the night before like shards of
broken glass, I realised the true horror of what had happened.
It was devastating. It was a familiar devastation; in 2008 I had
been hospitalised three times with alcohol poisoning. But this
was worse. Much worse.

In July 2009, I collapsed on stage at the Queensland
Performing Arts Centre in front of a packed crowd of four
hundred paying ticketholders. The night before, I had
performed the same stand-up routine and after the gig,

I caught up with a couple of friends from Alice who were in town. When I say, 'caught up', I mean, 'drank stupid amounts of vodka and had a raging all-nighter'. In the early hours of the morning, a cold shiver of realisation ran through my body. I knew I had two options: crawl under the doona and fight the horrors or stay awake and keep drinking. At that point, I wasn't the captain of the ship anymore, and the pirate who had hijacked my body chose the latter option. When I stepped on stage, I was in total blackout. I had no idea how drunk I was. I don't remember my head hitting the polished stage floor or the gasps of the shocked audience members. I don't remember the ambulance sirens or anyone checking for a pulse.

At the hospital, I found out I had been admitted with a blood alcohol reading of 0.44. That's nearly nine times the legal driving limit. That's enough to kill a truck driver. That's enough to make even a seasoned alcoholic collapse. The incident occurred seventy-two hours prior to my debut on the prime-time Channel 7 TV show *Dancing with the Stars* where two million viewers were expected to tune in. I was angry at myself, broken and frightened. More than anything, I had an absolute sense of being caught with my hand in the cookie jar and with crumbs all over me.

I'd had close calls before, but never been caught red-handed publicly. I felt like all the water in the world wouldn't quench my thirst. My agent and Channel 7 wanted to release a statement saying I was suffering from exhaustion and that's what made me collapse on stage (rather than all the vodka I'd consumed in the twenty-four hours preceding). I didn't want to join the throngs of 'exhausted' celebrities. I thought going public with my addiction would help. I could finally name it and own it. I had never considered speaking publicly about my problem before, but the incident forced my hand; and the idea of outing myself filled me with relief. Alcoholism is a heavy burden to carry around every minute of every day and I was ready to drop it like a potato sack and be free.

So I did, and I was. For a little while, at least. I explained to the kids I was an alcoholic and I was trying to get better. I think they were relieved, more than anything. My mum was confused by my public admission, and my dad was just sad for me. One of my sisters told me they noticed Dad sitting in his chair with tears in his eyes, saying softly under his breath, 'Poor Fiona.' In my first interview after the fall, I said, 'I was a monster lying dormant for years. There has been a lot of denial – for a long time. I tried to kid myself I was managing it, but I was a train crash about to happen.

After the fall, I knew I had no choice but to come out and admit I was an alcoholic. I feel very, very lucky that I had this hugely public wake-up call. Otherwise, I hate to think how I could've ended up.'

Dancing with the Stars was a welcome distraction from the dormant monster. I hit the jackpot with my dance partner Craig Monley. Besides being one of the kindest human beings on Earth, Craig is a goddamned Adonis! I had forgotten entirely what a young man felt like, and he was made up of nothing but muscle and good looks. I skipped to rehearsals every day, partly to see Craig in his tights, and also because I genuinely enjoyed the training. I was the fittest I'd ever been – and sober. I felt like a new woman, well, mostly …

*

My birthday was three weeks after 'the incident', as my sister Cate delighted in calling it. My parents were in Melbourne where I was filming *Dancing with the Stars*, completely sober, resisting the urge to go back to my hotel room every night and raid the mini-bar. Mum wanted to organise a birthday celebration for me, and even though I couldn't think of anything worse, I felt I didn't have any right to say no. I'd put them all through enough, I could suck it up for a night, even if I was still shaking with withdrawals.

Mum booked a table at a wine bar in South Yarra. Yes, Mum chose to host my birthday dinner at a bar stocked full of vices and temptation, three weeks after I had admitted to the entire country I was an alcoholic. I wish I was joking. I think it was hard for my family to fully understand my disease and what I was going through.

I sat with white knuckles and watched my family and friends celebrate my birthday, while I sipped soda water and smiled through clenched teeth, steering well clear of the alluring dark wood and green tiles of the bar. I left the dinner at the first opportunity. Leaving a party early felt entirely unnatural to me; it still does, to be honest. I was usually the one ordering another round of shots. I was the life of the party, not the killjoy. But I know now I can't wait around to be tempted. It's like that saying: if you sit in a barber shop long enough, you're going to get a haircut. And I didn't need a trim.

There's another saying: big drinkers give alcoholics a bad name. Big drinkers can drink heavily, but they have the power to put the bottle down. Alcoholics don't have any power. Big drinkers can have a few beers and still know they'll end up in their own bed later that night. Alcoholics can't make any assurances after the first sip. Big drinkers can have a blowout and still be in control. Alcoholics surrender their control to their disease, powerless against the kryptonite grip of a bottle of Smirnoff.

I know that many people look at alcoholics and think, *Why don't you just stop?* I sure did when I looked at my alcoholic uncle through younger eyes. It's easy to judge, and harder to empathetically walk in someone else's shoes and try to understand. The unfortunate reality is, alcoholism is a disease of the mind and body. You can't trust your thinking. It's the only disease that will actively tell you that you don't have a disease. It will whisper sweet nothings in your ear: 'It's only one drink, go on. You can just have a sip, take the edge off. It's not like you're breaking any laws. Don't be a sook. It won't kill you.' You want to believe the whispered lies, but as soon as you start engaging with the voice in your head, you lose. The voice always wins. And, eventually, the alcohol will kill you.

*

When I returned home to Alice, I discovered letters my daughter Mary-Agnes had written a year earlier when she was eleven. She had wanted me to find them far sooner than I did.

ALCOHOLICS

by Mary O'Loughlin

There is no cure to this bad, life-ruining disease, there is only absence. Alcoholics need to learn that their life is being taken over by alcohol, and that humans are much stronger than alcohol, which means they can live without it.

ABOUT LIVING WITH AN ALCOHOLIC

by Mary O'Loughlin

My mum is an alcoholic (although she denies it) and I hate it. Last year Mum told me that she would give up drinking for a year so then she might be a normal drinker again. I knew it was too good to be true, so to make her try and keep the promise I made her a locket with 'I love you' on one side and 'Promise' on the other. It only lasted until Christmas. Mum doesn't go out drinking all the time, but when she does, she gets really, really drunk. Every time I see her drunk, I cry, but I don't know exactly why. Either I need help, Mum needs help, or we both need help.

Reading it felt like a sucker punch to the stomach. I had tried to convince myself that I'd shielded my kids from my addiction. I told myself I didn't have the luxury of being an active alcoholic in front of five kids. When I was at home with them, I would white-knuckle it for weeks without touching a drop. My kids certainly weren't raised by someone under the influence. I laughingly referred to Alice as the Betty Ford Clinic. But alcoholics slip up, even at Betty Ford. And kids are smart, you can't hide the truth from them. They noticed the missed flights coming home from gigs, too smashed to get out of bed when the alarm went off. They saw me as a messy drunk after a big Friday night entertaining at home. They heard the vomiting after last call at Bojangles Nightclub. I didn't get away with as much as I thought I did. Mary-Agnes's notes were proof of that.

She was dead right, my Mary-Agnes, and to this day she's a watchdog of her own mental health. Four out of five of my kids go to counsellors like they go to the dentist. Knowing that I needed help, I committed to going to Alcoholics Anonymous. I was under no illusion; sitting in the Alice Springs church community centre on a stiff plastic chair surrounded by the broken and the defenceless, I knew I was exactly where I belonged. Still, the comedian in me got a kick out of the absurdity of humanity.

'Hello, my name is Sarah! And I am an alcoholic,' said a young girl. Polite clapping ensued, applause for the self-confessed drunk at an AA meeting. My internal monologue was cheering, *Well done, Sarah! Good on you! You've fucked up big time!*

Encouraged by our clapping, Sarah continued. 'I first realised that I had a problem with alcohol about a year ago.'

For heaven's sake, you look eighteen! I doubt you'd even know whether you were a vegetarian yet, let alone an alcoholic.

'My boyfriend and I went out to Bojangles Nightclub and we got very drunk.'

Been there, done that, sweet child, 374 times, give or take a hangover or two.

'We had a terrible fight and then went home, and the fight got worse and I threw the phone book at his head.'

Well, the Alice Springs phone book is hardly an encyclopaedia, I can't imagine it did much damage.

'Luckily it missed his head, but it was my wake-up call to finally do something about my drinking.'

Good for you, Sarah. Nip it in the bud. Meanwhile, thanks to your skills as a raconteur, I've never needed a double scotch more.

I leaned over to the gentleman to my left, and said, 'Excuse me, is there a higher level? I think I might be in the beginners' class.'

Since going public with my alcoholism, I was doing all the right things, going to meetings, having counselling and checking in with my recovery group. But no one tells you that once you admit you're an alcoholic, you're on your own. It's not like other life-threatening illnesses, people don't check in on you or drop off home-baked lasagnes. You don't have anyone lining up to hold your hand at AA like they would for a cancer patient going to a chemo appointment.

I remember going to my first social event in Alice after 'the incident'. It was an exhibition opening at a gallery in the Todd Mall. I was the designated driver and asked Chris to stay close to me. I was nervous. With recovery, you take giant steps everywhere you turn. Going to an event surrounded by free-flowing alcohol and people who knew I was a drunk felt like taking an enormous leap over a chasm filled with snapping crocodiles. When we arrived at the gallery, I felt the eyes of the room on me and went to reach for Chris's hand, but he was distracted and had moved away as we walked through the door. I knew then that he didn't understand. Maybe he didn't have to understand. My alcoholism had already hurt him, I think he had taken as much as he could take.

In hindsight I had set myself up to fail by outing myself. As much as I wanted to be, I was nowhere near ready for recovery. Speaking my truth had trapped me in a deep well of shame and lies, on my own, with no ladder to climb out and no rescue team on the way. It was enough to make an alcoholic drink.

*

At my first Melbourne International Comedy Festival show as an out (and not proud) alcoholic, I took the piss out of myself and my disease. 'Look, I don't want to brag,' I opened, 'but this is my first sober Melbourne Comedy Festival. I feel like I'm on *The Oprah Winfrey Show* ... Um, here's the thing, I am an alcoholic, which means, sadly for me, that I can never drink again forever. The real kicker is that I'm also Catholic and married, which is also forever. And now I have to do him sober.' Uproarious laughter.

'At the beginning, I just used to drink too much and be a bit loud at dinner parties. Alcoholism is a slow progression,' I continued. 'We'd invite dickheads over for dinner parties and I'd have to drink myself stupid just to put up with them.'

I turned my alcoholism into a gag, squeezing the monster for material. As I laughed it off, the monster was still lying dormant, hiding out of sight, waiting to return with a vengeance.

I saw my friend Dom Irrera backstage at a Sydney Comedy Festival gala not long after. 'Hey, I Googled you. You're breaking my heart. What's going on with you?' he asked, standing in my dressing room. 'I tell you what, after this we'll find a nice restaurant, then we'll order a nice bottle of wine and talk about your drinking problem.' God, I love comedians.

*

It sounds ridiculous now, but part of me wished I had a mental illness. Having depression or a personality disorder seemed far more showbiz and more fashionable than being a drunk. I thought a mental-health diagnosis would be more palatable, less disgusting and easier to digest. Perhaps people would be more forgiving and understanding if they thought of alcoholism as the disease it is.

At one stage, I was diagnosed with bipolar and I dined out on that wholeheartedly for weeks. I was prescribed a little purple pill, and what that medication did to me was horrifying. I almost lost my mind while trying to fix my mind. It was as though the tablet slowed everything down. One second felt like five minutes. I was hyper aware of everything: the feeling of the leather seat I was sitting on, my breathing, the number of times I blinked. I couldn't escape into a book or a TV show,

I was trapped in my own existence – and let me tell you, that's a very boring place to be.

I was on the drug for six months and when I finally stopped taking it, I went back to normal. Well, as 'normal' as I ever was. It turns out that even though I do experience higher highs and lower lows than a lot of people, so too does about 20 per cent of the population. I am just an ordinary alcoholic with heightened emotions. Bummer.

*

After the incident, my sobriety lasted about a year. Then I relapsed, and I relapsed hard. Returning to the bottle is the ultimate betrayal. It's this all-consuming feeling of letting everyone down, once again. From 2010 to 2019, I relapsed every three months like clockwork, and it got uglier each time, much uglier. No one who relapses is having a couple of glasses of red wine with dinner a week later. And in my case, there's no such thing as a quiet relapse. It's always loud and obnoxious. Like the drunkest bloke at the pub on a Friday night, fittingly. It's as though I need to drink the town dry to make it worth my while. Alcohol retards my thoughts completely, along with my behaviours and choices. And the fallout is severe.

After a relapse I would spend days in a state of desperation and deep depression. I would be paralysed with agoraphobia and couldn't leave the house or answer the phone. The clean-up after a relapse was exhausting, it's like you've flooded your house emotionally and need to rip up all the carpet and start again. I knew I was doing serious damage to myself physically and mentally, but I couldn't stop. I was powerless. I was nothing. Every time I relapsed, I would drop to my knees and pray for help. I'd beg with my hands pressed together at my heart, 'Please God, please God, let this be the last time.'

I remember 'fessing up to my relapse at my recovery meeting, explaining all the reasons I had for turning to the bottle. 'I just couldn't cope anymore, so I drank.'

The woman sitting across from me looked me dead in the eye and said, 'Dogs bark.' Dogs bark and alcoholics drink, the two certainties in life. It reminded me of a quote my grandmother used to repeat, 'See eggshells, suspect eggs.' My eggshells were empty vodka bottles.

It was always the same thing that pushed me off the wagon, a spiral of self-hate, fear and selfishness. The voice in my head would remind me of all the pain I'd caused because of my drinking and convince me the only remedy to the inner dialogue of abuse was, you guessed it, more drinking. As soon as I engaged with the voice in my head, I lost. The voice always wins. It was an irresistible solution, a quick fix, a single twist to open a bottle of vodka and make the voice shut up. But the hard truth is, the answer is not and will never be in another drink.

Often, it was my phone that triggered a relapse. The thought of having to call my mum and put on a smiley voice, made my hands shake so much I couldn't dial her number. I was scared of sounding miserable, which I was, so I'd have a couple of drinks to steady my voice and lubricate the conversation. It was the ultimate sign of weakness: needing Dutch courage to have a chat to your mum.

When I relapsed after a year of sobriety, I collapsed with shame and grief. I couldn't handle the guilt, so I lied. I told everyone I was still sober and that I had given up my pre-show shots. In fact, I told them I had swapped the ritual for something far more positive; instead of sneaking off to the bathroom to down vodka, I said I would read the letter Mary-Agnes wrote about my drinking. I lied and I lied as I rummaged through my bra to pull out my old-faithful two mini-bar bottles of Smirnoff in the toilet backstage.

I'd made a pact with the universe: I was allowed to keep drinking pre-show until I could earn enough money to take a year off work and book into a long-term rehab clinic. That's what I wanted more than anything, to be admitted to a 12-step program to check out of life for one year and focus on my sobriety. I was certain that's what I needed. I had even humiliated myself by calling wealthy relatives in the middle of the night, drunk, begging them for the money I would need. When they said no, I was broken. I didn't know what else to do, so I stuck to my pact. I pretended I was sober and continued to drink vodka in a locked toilet stall before shows.

I gave myself a hall pass to drink at gigs – and sometimes before, and sometimes after. When Mary-Agnes was fourteen, she came to Melbourne with me for a week when I had a few shows booked in. Before one of the gigs, I got legless and Mary-Agnes insisted on coming with me. 'You can't go out there like this on your own,' she said, swapping roles with me and being the parent. She was right. When I stepped on stage, I was slurring my words so embarrassingly, Mary-Agnes had to walk outside because she couldn't bear to watch. Thank God she did because I collapsed on stage and they escorted the audience out. I was taken to hospital and Mary-Agnes had to find somewhere to stay that night. She was *fourteen*.

*

I became a secret agent on tour. My mission? To source alcohol without giving up my cover. Every time I arrived in a country town, I would case the streets and make a plan of attack to get to a bottle shop, alone and unnoticed, so I could buy two mini bottles of Smirnoff. I'd go into bottle shops with a cap on, speaking in various accents. In one town, I'd be a posh English woman with money to burn after a long hard day of being rich and privileged, 'Ooh, just two mini bottles of Smirnoff, many thanks and best regards, fine sir.'

In the next town, I'd be an American tourist, with a husky Brooklyn drawl. 'I think my daughter said she wanted … Spirnoff, is that what it's called? They do shots, the kids. They have two of your little Spirnoffs and then they go out to the club.'

Sometimes, I would act like I was mute and pass them a note. No accent needed.

I committed to my characters to put the bottle-o staff off any scent that I was Fiona O'Loughlin, the alcoholic comedian doing a show at the local RSL that night. I don't think I needed to go to the lengths I did. I could have just shut up and bought the vodka, it probably would have been less conspicuous.

At festivals, I was safe if I went straight home after my show. But I didn't always stick to my self-imposed curfew, especially when mini bottles of vodka were involved. At the bar, surrounded by my peers who all thought I was on the wagon, I would pay another comic $50 or $100 to sneak me drinks. The comic was a heroin addict and we were each other's enablers. We were both at the height of our addictions and I knew I was wading into murky waters. By paying him to enable my addiction, I was enabling his. It struck me that I was a junkie just like him. I needed a fix. I thought I would die without it.

On tour, my biggest fear was always the bottle shop being closed or it not stocking the mini bottles. I could never plan ahead and stock up on vodka on tour because I couldn't be trusted with alcohol on me. If I had to buy a bigger bottle instead of my strict two-minis limit, I would pour out over half of the bottle, leaving just three standard drinks' worth. It was wasteful and ridiculous, but it was the only way I could stick to my pact. As soon as I completed my mission, and hid my target safely in my bra, I could relax. It was as exhausting as being a junkie, I imagine, just not quite as expensive (even when I was tipping vodka down the sink).

One night in late 2013, my worst nightmare came true. The BWS in an unremarkable country town I can't remember the name of didn't have mini bottles of vodka and I had no other option but to buy a half-bottle, 375mL. When I turned up to the gig drunk, my manager at the time, Anthony Menchetti, and support act, Andrea Powell, knew straightaway. I'd been caught. I smelled of alcohol and could barely stand up straight. My deep, dark, dirty secret had been exposed. They told me they were heartbroken. I knew how they felt. Oh God, I knew how they felt.

We had another show to do the following night in the next unremarkable country town and Anthony and Andrea watched me like hawks all day. I was beyond mortified and I knew I couldn't sneak off to the bottle-o in good conscience. So, I surrendered. For the first time in my career, I was going to step on stage stone cold sober. That morning, it felt like I woke in the gallows with a deathly hangover. It's hard to describe the morbid terror that clung to me that day. Every heavy step took me closer to my worst fear being realised. On stage, my hands were clammy against the cool microphone. I took the mask off, certain I would out myself as a fraud and horrify the audience with the ugly truth. I could hear the anticipated jeers and boos. *Get off the stage! You don't deserve to be here! You're not fooling anyone, stop kidding yourself!* I could see the *Daily Mail* headline already: 'Fiona O'Loughlin Exposes Herself as a Hideous Imposter

Beast'. I could feel the crushing humiliation – and I was so frightened.

To my total surprise, nothing happened. The world didn't end. It was a regular old gig. In fact, it was better than a regular old gig. I was funny and the crowd laughed. I did my job and they did theirs. I could not believe how wrong I had been. It was a beautiful revelation. I'd never known relief like it. It was like having an epidural during childbirth. The next day, waking up in the motel under the room's heavy blue quilt was like waking up from a nightmare. I felt like I'd finally stopped falling. I squealed into my hard pillow with glee and smiled all the way home like a sober lunatic.

I had won the battle; I had done a show sober and lived to tell the tale. And to this day, unless a gig caught me in the midst of a relapse, I have never used alcohol pre-show again.

I may have won the battle, but I was yet to win the war.

CHAPTER 4

AN UNRELIABLE WITNESS

I DIDN'T FOLLOW THE PROTOCOL THAT NIGHT. SINCE coming out as an alcoholic, I had put in place measures to protect myself from temptation at gigs: my team would remove the mini-bar from my hotel room and organise a driver to pick me up from the event straight after I walked off stage. It was in my contract that I would mingle for fifteen minutes with the crowd, then do an Irish goodbye, slipping away without telling anyone. One night in 2012 before I'd won the battle and performed sober for the first time, I emceed a corporate gig for a disability charity at Parliament House in Canberra.

With more than a decade of stand-up under my belt, I was in hot demand for emcee gigs. I'd just appeared on the second season of *The Celebrity Apprentice Australia* and was, by all accounts, a household name (even if I was the first contestant 'fired' on *The Apprentice*).

That night, the Canberra gig had gone phenomenally well, and the organiser was thanking me profusely. He was a gay man about my age who was dying of cancer; this was to be his last event. I was invested in making sure it was a great night for him, so when he told me a respected judge wanted to meet me after the gig, I agreed. I told my driver to leave, and said that I'd catch a taxi back to the hotel after I met the judge. That was my first mistake. And I made it willingly, knowing that I was immediately opening myself up to temptation.

On my way to the bathroom to fix my make-up before shaking the esteemed judge's hand, I passed an unaccompanied catering trolley full of champagne flutes, filled to the brim with bubbles of temptation. Temptation I couldn't resist. It was like that scene in the film *Flight* where Denzel Washington gazes at the mini bottles of Grey Goose through the glass of his hotel mini-bar and you think he's not going to do it, then he does. I downed three glasses on my way into the toilet, and three on the way out. That was my second mistake, and third and fourth and fifth and ... Dogs bark, and bark, and bark.

Part of me was flattered that a judge wanted to meet me, Fiona O'Loughlin from Warooka. Imagine that. Another part of me, the inner alcoholic, was always looking for a reason to relapse – and free unattended champagne proved to be an impossible test. I told myself I was doing it for the organiser who was dying of cancer. By staying at the event and meeting the judge, I was basically fulfilling the bloke's last dying wish. Who was I to deny him that?

After six champagne flutes, I was hilariously witty and charming with the judge. The organiser couldn't have been happier with me. I'd gone above and beyond to make his final event a roaring success. It was another reason to stay and enjoy the night, another excuse to drink on the sly, another excuse to lie to myself.

When the event wrapped up, a group of women were going to kick on in the wild city of Canberra and invited me to join them. 'Oh no, I can't. I don't drink,' I said, already flying.

The group insisted. 'Oh, Jeanene's our sober driver for the night, she'll drink orange juice with you.'

My last memory is of sitting in the outdoor area of a city establishment, slipping the waiter $20 and $50 notes to put lots of vodka in my orange juice. From there, it's only vague flashes. Waving goodbye to the women when they call it a night at a decent hour because they are normal people in control of their actions. Flash. Sitting in the gutter outside a club with a young couple smoking cigarettes and talking shit, sharing my slurred life wisdom. Flash. Going to an ATM and withdrawing cash, too much cash. Flash. I don't remember how I got back to my hotel or unlocking the door to my soulless room with grey carpet and charred black timber finishes.

My next flash of memory is waking up in my hotel room in the dark early hours of the morning. There's someone on top of me and inside me. I don't know if my underpants are on the carpet discarded by the side of the bed or scrunched up between the sheets. I know I didn't take them off. I pass back out in the darkness; dark sky, dark timber, dark memories.

In the light of the morning, I wake with a sense of dread and a foul taste in my mouth. The memory of what happened in the darkness comes rushing back to me. When I see the stranger next to me in bed, it's like a bolt of realisation. I know I have altered my life forever. Nothing will ever be the same. What has happened, can never be undone.

It's only after I've contemplated the enormity of the situation that I think about my safety. I don't know who this person is, what he's capable of or how he'll act when he wakes up. My internal safety debriefing is interrupted by the blaring noise of the phone ringing on the bedside table. I've missed my flight home to Alice Springs.

'No, I'm not drinking,' I tell Chris, lying through my furry teeth. 'Of course I'm not drinking, I just slept in.'

By now the stranger is sitting up in bed. I consider my options and decide the safest bet is to act completely normal and gauge if he is a serial killer or a regular bloke thinking he's had a one-night stand. I start talking to him and bitching about my husband for waking us up. I know I have to get the stranger out of the room, and I think the easiest way to do that is to chat to him as though he is supposed to be there.

What I didn't know was that I hadn't hung up the phone properly, and Chris was listening to every word I spoke to the stranger in my bed.

After making small talk with the stranger, I realise I'm not in mortal danger. He's not particularly threatening, so I forcefully ask him to leave.

I must have given the stranger my number because later on that dreadful day, my phone buzzes with a blatant text: *I'm not a bad man.*

So much about that time doesn't make sense. As unreliable a witness as I am, I stayed awake for nights afterwards. My pupils like saucers. My memories like shards of glass – cutting me when I reach for them.

*

I've never called it rape. Sometimes words are safer left unspoken. Even though there's no way I could have consented to having sex because I was passed out, I'm not a reliable witness to what happened that night. I have no memory of how the stranger ended up in my hotel room, in my bed, inside me. For all I know, he could have been a raging alcoholic himself, on a bender, not in control of his actions.

I've never thought of myself as a rape victim. When it happened, I figured I had enough to be sad about already. There was no room in my heart to afford myself any comfort. I was the one who put myself in that situation. I was the one who relapsed. I was the one who got blackout drunk and opened the door to danger. I may not have deserved what happened, but I didn't deserve any tears of sympathy either.

After I got the stranger out the door, I spiralled. Chris rang me back after the man left and told me he'd heard everything.

I didn't leave that grey, soulless room for twenty-four hours or more. My manager came from Sydney to sort out the hotel bill and check up on me. He told me later that I seemed 'drug affected', which confused me, until I remember the flash of being at an ATM withdrawing cash ... way too much cash.

I was also terrified that I would be pregnant. Once upon a time, I would have considered myself pro-life. It was easy for me to be against abortion when I was a middle-class married Catholic woman living on the bright side of the road. After that night, I crossed the road and never looked back. If the pregnancy test had shown a positive cross, I would have – without a doubt – terminated the pregnancy. I had already planned to do so before I peed on the stick. I was becoming more unrecognisable to myself with every passing day.

*

The flight I missed was to Alice Springs, where I was meant to meet Chris and travel with him down to Adelaide to host a Pink Ribbon Ball. It was the flashest event of the year in Adelaide; everybody who was anyone was attending. I flew straight to Adelaide, Chris met me at the Hyatt Regency on North Terrace, where we had a pre-booked suite.

Whilst waiting at the departure gate in Canberra, I recognised a trio of familiar heads in front of me. 'Well, well, well, what a pack of arseholes,' I teased.

Steven Gates, Scott Edgar and Simon Hall from the musical comedy group Tripod all turned around and laughed. 'What have you been up to, O'Loughlin?' they asked, clocking my dishevelled state or maybe smelling the alcohol on my breath.

We had toured together over the years and shared galas and stages on both sides of the globe. Gatesy and I had been very tight friends for years and I filled him in on the last few days of my life. I didn't leave anything out. Reliving my horrific flashes of memory, I got back what I always did from my carnival family: deep concern. Gatesy hugged me goodbye that morning at the airport in Canberra, or as I like to call our capital city, the scene of the crime. It was the last hug I would have for a long time.

In Adelaide, Chris couldn't speak to me or look at me after what he'd heard on the phone. He was convinced I was having a full-blown affair with this bloke in Canberra. Someone had told him, 'You must never forgive her.' And he didn't. Every time I tried to talk to him about what had happened, he shut me down and refused to listen.

I was utterly shattered – and hadn't stopped drinking since Canberra. I'd mounted up so many intolerable memories, I didn't have space for any more. I wanted to black out and stay blacked out. There was only one option: I knew I just had to get through the Ball and then I could kill myself. I didn't know how, but I was working on a plan. I performed at the Pink Ribbon Ball completely shit-faced. I remember what I spat in Chris's eye not long before I passed out, like an Elizabeth Taylor character, 'I'm never saying sorry until I am.'

The next morning, I woke up alone. Chris had left early to play golf. In the suite, I had access to insurmountable amounts of alcohol in the bar and on speed dial from room service, and I knew what I had to do. I was going to get impossibly drunk and drown myself in the bathtub. I drew a bath and drank as much as I could, in the hope that I would pass out, sink under the water and die. I felt like I had made a mess so big that I couldn't clean it up, ever. I was desperate to end it; so desperate, the thought of Chris finding my body didn't enter my mind. Nor did the idea of my kids attending my funeral. I chugged Grey Goose from the bottle and willed myself to slip under the water. I did pass out a number of times, but I kept waking up in a cold bath with my head above water. For fuck's sake. I refilled the tub with warm water again and again. Then I forced myself under the rim and held my breath, only to involuntarily surface for air. Drowning yourself is the hardest thing to do. Every time I came up for air, I hated myself. How pathetic, weak, useless could one person be? I was nothing, less than nothing.

When it became apparent I wasn't going to be able to end the misery in the bathtub, I called my sister Cate and said, 'I've been trying to kill myself all day. Can you help me?'

I was admitted to the Adelaide Clinic. It was my first time in a psychiatric ward, and it was pure bliss. I was safe. I was at the stage where I just couldn't do life. I didn't have to at the clinic. I was there for a month, being looked after, eating properly and not drinking alcohol. I started learning about my own psychology and the psychology of my disease. I was an eager student; it was a pity I couldn't apply the principles to my own life.

I didn't see or hear from Chris while I was at the clinic. When I was discharged, I found out life in Alice Springs would never be the same again. Chris had told the kids. He'd told everybody. It seemed as if the whole town knew. I didn't try to defend myself. I was too ashamed. I told my brother-in-law and his wife the full story. I think I blew the lid off their Sunday afternoon. I didn't hide the fact that I was drunk that night, I just told them what happened. They said, 'Thank you. We hope you're okay,' and changed the subject. I explained to the kids what I remembered and didn't bring it up again. Years later I was talking to Mary-Agnes about sexual assault and told her I was still confused about what had happened in Canberra. In my mind, it was as grey as the hotel room carpet.

When I stepped through the door to our family home after a month in the clinic, I was a stranger. I slept on a mattress on the living-room floor. It was a heinous time and I can't remember exactly how long it lasted. I begged, I pleaded. I cooked, I cleaned. I tried to act like everything was normal, but it wasn't. And I wasn't kidding anyone. At that point, Mary-Agnes was our only kid still at home – Bert was at boarding school – and as much as I tried to shield her from our marriage breakdown, I doubt I did. As the kids got older, they saw the crack in our relationship widen and heard the ensuing rockslides.

The Catholic in me couldn't even comprehend the thought of divorce. Growing up, the only person I knew with a failed marriage was an uncle on my dad's side and we knew nothing about it. Divorce was high on the list of things we didn't talk about at the dinner table.

Over the years, I'd always promised the kids they never had to worry about divorce – that's how confident I was about staying married, despite all our struggles. I desperately wanted to get Bert and Mary-Agnes through to eighteen with married parents. I thought, *We've come this far.* But we couldn't go any further. Our relationship was over.

I told the kids if they wanted to have a cry about me and their dad, they should listen to Mary Black's 'The Loving Time'. I must have shed a bucket full of tears to that song, it spoke to me and captured the haunting loss of a marriage breakdown.

It reads like a fairytale and that's what it was
Young man in his prime
young girl from a cross
The most perfect of strangers
and then the night closed in
and the holy ground took care of everything
Now she was a fine one
and he was a handsome man
One look was enough and away they ran
They spend many happy hours
and then the night closed in

and the holy ground took care of everything

Oh what's the use in complaining?

In for a penny, in for a pound

I remember the loving time

and nothing else really counts

And I recall the promise they made

With a faith I can but admire

That she'd be the one he adored

and he'd be her heart's desire

It didn't come true in the end

they went their separate ways

He couldn't change what he was

she wasn't ready to wait

They couldn't live in the daylight

they let the night close in

and the holy ground took care of everything

I remember the loving time

and nothing else really counts

At some point, I travelled back to Warooka to tell my dad what had happened, and that Chris and I were separating. I thought, if I could square off with Dad, I could square off the whole ordeal with myself. Before I arrived, I played the anticipated scene over and over in my mind. The look of horror I expected to see on Dad's face haunted me. I practised what I was going to say so much that I had memorised it like a best man's speech.

'I was blackout drunk and woke up with a man in my bed,' I told him, reliving the shame.

Dad was absolutely beautiful. He just held my hand and squeezed it reassuringly.

Nick was also a great comfort to me (and Chris) during our marriage breakdown. He was there for both of us, but he didn't take sides. If Chris started to vent, Nick would tell him, 'I can't listen to that, she's the mother of your children.' And he'd repeat the same phrase to me (except he'd say father, not mother – obviously). Nick and I laughed on the phone together one day about Chris's big mouth. For all his faults, Chris O'Loughlin is not a malevolent person. He would have been an open book at his local football club, Feds, where he dropped into most evenings. Feds had always been like the Cheers bar of Alice Springs, where everyone knew your name.

'He's like Steve Carell in *Crazy, Stupid, Love*,' I said to Nick.

'He's just blowing off steam, Fiona.'

'Yeah, I know, I get it.' God knows I'd blown off plenty of steam regarding Chris over the years, mostly to Nick and

Jasmin. They were true friends to both of us – and God we needed them.

*

While one blackout night in Canberra was the final nail in the coffin, the breakdown of my marriage was a drawn-out affair. Emphasis on the word 'affair'. After the Butch saga, Chris had accused me of cheating on him again and again over the years, and finally here we were. I was the disgusting alcoholic who had fucked a stranger and torn our family apart.

But until that grey night in 2012, my nose had been clean. At least physically. Or had it? There's a sea of desperate and drunk kisses. Tawdry lip locks I'd buried in my hidden hall of shame. After I formed such a close connection with Butch, I became open to the idea of having an emotional affair, and actively sought them out to fill the void in my humourless marriage. I figured, if I was going to be accused of something anyway, I may as well get some enjoyment out of it. I flirted uncontrollably when I was away, acting very much like a single woman, especially when I was drinking. It must have been painful for Chris. I was out of control. To put it mildly, I was a cunt to him. I had matched his sins and then some.

I developed a textual relationship with an English comedian in the mid-2000s. He's a brilliant stand-up and one of my favourites. He's fifteen years younger, and at first I was blind to his schoolboy crush on me. I didn't see myself as anything, let alone the object of someone's affection.

My English friend and I would make each other laugh over text messages, sparring and ribbing each other. It was pure banter, a delicious escape from my stale life as a housewife in Alice Springs. One day I was changing the sheets and when I flipped the mattress, I found reams and reams of paper – print-offs of my texts. I sat on the edge of the unmade bed, shocked at the invasion of my privacy, but even more shocked about how Chris had managed to print off text messages. He was hardly a tech genius. I even wondered if he had hired a private detective to investigate me, that's how much I doubted his tech skills. Chris never confronted me about it. I was a ball of guilt, regardless. I knew what I was doing was wrong, but I couldn't stop it.

*

The drive from our house to the Alice Springs airport takes twenty minutes, following the dry bed of the Todd River, passing the turn-off to the sewerage works, the racecourse and a never-ending stream of road trains. The highway cuts through the MacDonnell Ranges, which surround the city like a gilded fence. The rocky edges of the East and West Ranges stand tall at Heavitree Gap like guards. Every time I drove through The Gap, I felt a sense of excitement and nostalgia; leaving the comforts of home is always equal parts thrilling and nerve-wracking. Interestingly, Heavitree Gap is a sacred site for Indigenous men. In the past, women were not allowed to pass through The Gap and had to climb over the Ranges. Some elder women still bow their heads and are silent when passing through to show respect. I was silent this time too, consumed with sadness and defeat.

Chris was driving me to the airport for a corporate gig in Melbourne and I knew I wasn't coming back. Ever. I'd only packed a carry-on bag for a two-night stay, but on the twenty-minute drive, I made the decision to leave Alice Springs for good. Chris and I argued on the highway. The same old scratched record that we'd played over and over again for twenty-seven years. Chris started driving faster, which terrified me. I screamed at him to slow down. The end was no surprise to either of us. It smelled like burned rubber. Kasey Chambers' song 'The Captain' played in the background.

*

Chris and I still aren't legally divorced, even though we've been separated for eight years. I wouldn't even know where to begin with getting a divorce. And I think a part of me still can't imagine not being married to him. In many ways, this is the perfect marriage, living totally separate lives. There are many things I regret in my life, but you can never regret anything that led to your children. I know deep in my soul that Chris and I were meant to have those kids together. And if I hadn't married him, I would have probably fantasised about what could have been for the rest of my life.

Our financial separation was graceful and a moment in time that Chris and I can be forever proud of. Our home had been mortgaged to capacity and all Chris had was his physical ability to forge on and his superannuation.

'The kids can't lose the house,' I cried through my mobile phone to Chris. We had obviously been advised to get lawyers, but I knew that Christopher O'Loughlin, Mr Can Do, was the only person I trusted when it came down to what was fair.

'Fiona, it's all I have, but I can give you the super,' he told me, explaining that we couldn't withdraw it yet, but it would be my nest egg.

'Thank you, Chris,' I said as relief flooded through me. The kids were sad, of course, but ultimately, they were as relieved as we were. Tess later said on my *Australian Story* episode, 'For the two younger kids, Bert and Mary, I can see how confused they were at the time. But for Henry, Biddy and myself, I think we all agreed that it was a much healthier decision for Mum to leave Alice Springs and for Mum and Dad to go their separate ways.'

The end was as simple as the beginning back in 1985 at the Yorketown Catholic Church. And for me, it was just as moving.

CHAPTER 5

'JUNE NORTHERN'

ELBOURNE WAS A FRESH START, A CLEAN SLATE, A new beginning. For all of about two weeks. After leaving Alice Springs for good, I moved into a little flat in Prahran at the end of 2012, living with Tess, then twenty-four, and later Mary-Agnes, who was still in high school. I spent the last dollars in my bank account paying the bond and first month's rent. It was a nice enough art deco apartment with white walls and large windows, but it was on the corner of two busy roads and the constant noise of the traffic put me on edge. The feng shui was all off. Still, I made it my own with pretty furniture, my floral Laura Ashley armchair taking pride of place in the lounge room.

I was standing on the landing outside the flat when I answered a phone call advising me I owed the tax office $120 000. I almost fell to my knees. I couldn't even imagine what $120 000 looked like, let alone how I would access that much money. I'd always left my paperwork to my manager and Chris. Since one had left and the other had been separated from, I was high and dry with a mammoth tax bill I had to deal with on my own. Before we split, Chris and I had invested in a business that flopped and wiped out all of our retirement savings. Instead of starting again with a clean slate, I was starting with a $120 000 debt. Once again, I felt like I was drowning.

You know that burning feeling when your face turns bright red with shame? I woke up like that every day in Melbourne. My first thought of a morning was of the mess I had made of my life. Heat would rise up my chest and spread like wildfire across my cheeks. I'd run through the checklist of humiliations: I was broke, alone, desperate and a secret alcoholic pretending to be sober. Living such a hideous life, while maintaining a happy façade in front of my children and working non-stop to try to clear my debt, was bone-achingly exhausting. The pressure of trying to get my life together while hiding my deep, dark, dirty secret eventually broke me.

One of my lowest moments was being recognised in a Chapel Street pawn shop hocking my beautiful engagement ring. When I signed my name, the bloke behind the counter looked me up and down and said, 'Fiona O'Loughlin, as in, *the* Fiona O'Loughlin?' How's my luck! I rarely get recognised on the street; people don't realise how short I am, so I fly under the radar, literally. And there I was, spotted pawning my only valuable belonging so I could pay my rent and buy a bottle of vodka. It's incredible how expensive my addiction was. It's not just the alcohol itself, it was the cost of hospitalisation, the price of refunding cancelled show tickets, the loss of income when I was in hospital instead of on stage. There are no sick days in comedy. Just negative bank balances and bounced payments. Tess went to the Chapel Street pawn shop later and retrieved my ring.

In my quest to pay off my tax debt and keep funding my addiction, I performed a regional tour in South Australia with promoter Anthony Lamond. As we drove through the Southern Flinders Ranges, I stared forlornly out the window. Passing Mount Remarkable, I thought about Chris's mum, Geraldine, and sister Libby. That's where their plane crashed in

1980. The wreckage is still there. I sat in self-pity, holding on to my seatbelt for some kind of comfort. My co-dependency had played into my marriage to Chris. I wanted to fill the void left by his mother and sister, instead I added another gaping hole to his heart.

I'd fallen off the wagon the night before and was at the beginning stages of an epic bender. I didn't just fall off the wagon on that tour, my leg got caught in the wheel spokes and dragged me across the state until I was a bloody, battered mess.

When we arrived at the small town we were heading to for a gig, I proceeded to pour vodka on my self-pity and my jangled, jittery head. It was one of the worst shows I've ever done. I was incoherent. It will be the first stop on my 'Making Amends Tour'. My old school friends Angela and Gabriel were in the audience because they lived nearby. I can still feel the shame of someone having to escort me off stage. It was *that* bad. Angela took me back to her house with Gabriel, and Gabriel slept in the same bedroom as me to keep an eye on me. Angela was a winemaker, and in the middle of the night I snuck out of the room and slugged a bottle of red wine that I'd found in her kitchen. I was terribly ashamed, incredibly sick and very frightened knowing I had done the utterly unthinkable again. It was one of the most soul-destroying mornings of my life.

My sister Genevieve came and picked me up from Angela's house the next day; the silence between us was filled with familiar disappointment. My hands started shaking with withdrawals an hour into the drive back to Adelaide. The will to get more alcohol was a powerful force. I needed to keep the wolves at bay. My very life depended on it. I scanned the streets of every town we drove through for an open bottle shop or pub. When I saw one, I told Genevieve I had to go to the bathroom, urgently. She drove past the pub and pulled up at the public toilets in the main street of town. I hid in the toilet block until Genevieve looked away and then I bolted along the street to the pub. It was shut down; the windows were boarded up with wood. I was gutted. I snuck into a side street and knocked on a stranger's door. An old lady answered. 'I'm so sorry to bother you,' I said, 'but I'm on a road trip with my sister and I think I ate something "off" at breakfast, can I please use your bathroom?'

The poor old dear let me in straight away. I cased the joint for booze. In the hallway on the way to the bathroom was a full bar of liquor – a bottle of every spirit, neatly arranged from white to dark and meticulously dusted. I'd hit the jackpot. When the old lady was in the next room, I chugged as much as I could in the time it would have taken me to go to the bathroom. My hands were still shaking as I gulped down almost half a bottle.

Genevieve eventually tracked me down and took me back to the car. Shortly out of town it was apparent that I was rotten drunk. I lit up a cigarette, to Genevieve's disgust. 'Put the cigarette out, Fiona. You are not smoking in my car,' she said.

'Here's the thing, Genevieve, I *am* smoking in your car. It's happening right now. And I'm going to keep smoking all the way back to Adelaide. There's nothing you can do about it. So, save your whingeing for someone who cares,' I replied belligerently, blowing smoke into the air. I was hideous to her. I screamed at her because I knew I could. I was scared of myself.

Genevieve didn't respond to my ugliness. I looked out the window so I didn't have to see her crying.

For every story like this, there's at least five exactly the same that I don't know about. Maybe I was blackout drunk or maybe I've suppressed the memory so far within my soul I can't reach it anymore, but I'm always waiting for my buried humiliations to come back and haunt me. In every country town where I've relapsed, there's a folklore legend about me. One day I went into the newsagency of another regional town in South Australia and the bloke behind the counter said, 'It's good to see you back in town. Jake will be thrilled.'

'Who's Jake?'

Apparently, I'd got so drunk after my last gig there, I missed the last train to Adelaide and Jake drove me all the way back. God love Jake.

*

My first summer holidays without Chris were a mess. Or rather, I was a mess. I spent the Christmas break in South Australia with my kids visiting family. We stayed at Cate and Phil's family beach house on Horseshoe Bay in Port Elliot. It's one of those posh beachside destinations where everyone has the same blue-and-white striped sunshades. I thought they must have been council issued there were so many of them, so I found a free one and set myself up under it. I was enjoying the serenity until 'Jane' came storming across the sand to inform me I was sitting in her tent, turning her snobby nose up at me. It was like a scene out of *Kath & Kim* with Prue and Trude.

That night, we all had dinner at a pub in town with Cate and her family. I was secretly drinking vodka until it wasn't a secret anymore. I got drunk and made a fool of myself. Same old shit. My kids were there and saw me in all my alcoholic glory, the very glory I had tried to shield them from for all those years.

When I woke up the next morning – predictably feeling like death – I went for a walk with my sister to escape my embarrassment. A few paces down the street, a man dropped dead in front of me. I started doing CPR on him and screamed out to Cate for help. I pounded on his chest and Cate gave him mouth-to-mouth – it was like a scene from *Grey's Anatomy*. I was desperate to revive him. I wouldn't be surprised if I screamed, 'Don't you die on me, you bastard!' I thought that if only I could save him, I could redeem myself. If only he could take another breath, all my sins would be forgiven. If only. The man turned a deathly shade of purple and I stopped doing compressions. An ambulance took his body away, and I went back to the house in shock. I couldn't stop seeing it.

Henry drove us from Port Elliot to Warooka, where we stayed with my brother Richard, again at Cletta. I sat in the passenger seat and cracked open a half-bottle of Smirnoff. I was beyond trying to shield my kids from my disease. Bert looked at me in horror as I drank defiantly.

'You have an alcoholic mother, get over it. This is what it looks like,' I said.

Henry calmly pulled the car over to the side of the road. 'If you don't stop now,' he said, 'I will take you back to Adelaide.'

I put the bottle down. It was a moment of madness and remains a horrible memory. I have a lot of terrible memories from that time in my life.

During that summer, I took the kids to the Bottom End, the tip of the Yorke Peninsula fringed with beautiful beaches and lush national park. Biddy was in London and she called when I was driving, so we put her on speaker phone. 'Does Dad have a girlfriend?' she asked. Those five words took my breath away. It felt like I had been winded. I tried to keep a straight face while I fell apart on the inside. The end of a marriage is traumatic, but the finality of your ex moving on with someone else is truly brutal. I don't know what I expected. That we'd stay trapped in our marriage? That we would somehow make things better? I was just so sad for us both, but tried to hide that from the kids.

While in Warooka, I went to the Parish House with my brother Richard, a practising Catholic. He was marrying and wanted to ask the priest about the formalities.

When we sat down at the Parish House, the priest opened a bottle of champagne and poured us all a glass. 'Sorry, Father, I can't drink that,' I said.

'Why not?'

'I'm an alcoholic.'

'We are all alcoholics, Fiona.'

It was the green light I needed. Who was I to argue with a man of God? I could hardly turn down his gracious offer. It would have been rude. And everyone knows I'd rather be dead than rude, so I raised the glass. And another. And another. And ... my last memory was scrounging around my great-grandfather's house at 4 am drinking a bottle of port I'd found at the back of a cupboard that was probably as old as him.

The next day, I heard my mum on the phone to a relative. 'Well, we had an incident here with Fiona last night,' she said. I bowed my head. Tess came into my room and I was incredibly cruel to her. I threw my pain in her face. 'You have no idea how hard my life is. You don't know what I've been through. You won't ever be able to understand what it's like,' I hissed, as though I were the only person in the world who had issues.

There is nothing I regret more than the hurt I've caused my children. I can still hear the ugly things I've said to them in rare but awful moments of madness. I can still see the sadness on their faces. I can still feel their throbbing ache for a different mother, a better mother, a sober mother.

I'm not a confrontational person, but when I'm on a bender, I shape up like a fighter competing for the title of Worst Family Member. With a gut full of alcohol, I used to call my siblings up on the phone to blame them for all of my troubles, to drag them over the hot coals of our past, to throw my pain at them. The things I've said to my sisters in drunken rages are hideous. They were the only people I could fight with – and I did, loudly and obnoxiously.

*

It was a selfish thought. But I was so weary, I truly believed I would be better as a memory. There were no more good memories for me to make, for anyone, ever. It was time to call it a day before things got even worse and my memory was further tarnished. John Mayer's 'Slow Dancing in a Burning Room' was the soundtrack for my self-pity.

Sitting in my room in Prahran in 2013, I pulled out the power cord from my vacuum cleaner and wrapped it around my neck. Tight. I pressed the recoil button, hoping the cord would retract and choke me to death. It didn't work. On to Plan B ...

I booked into Hotel Saville on Commercial Road in South Yarra under the alias 'June Northern'. It was a hideous brown-brick octagonal hotel with green carpet and heavy drapes. My plan was to not walk out of that hotel. I stopped by the chemist on my way there and bought a packet of benzodiazepines to go with my bottle of vodka. Always a bottle of vodka. I was intent on ending my life, I'd never been more intent about anything. I was sober when I made the decision, unlike the last time, so I meant business. I lay down on the bed of my hotel room and called it a day.

*

I have an almost psychic connection with my youngest daughter, Mary-Agnes, my last precious baby. It's like our psyches are still joined by an invisible umbilical cord. I wrote this letter to her the night before she was born and have treasured it ever since ...

Dear you,

It's Tuesday night, 29th of July.

The night before you are born. We are at Uncle Tim's

house, you, me, Dad, Henry and Bert. Biddy and Tess are

in Alice Springs and very excited to hear who you are in the

morning.

I already know who you are. I can't wait to hold you and kiss your face. I've loved you since I first knew that you were coming.

I don't know if you're a boy or a girl, but I know who you are, little you.

Part of me is sad tonight, most of me is happier than I've ever been.

But I'll miss you. You are probably my last baby and I'll treasure every kick and nudge.

I never want to forget what it felt like to have you inside of me.

You're asleep now and I think I'll join you soon.

I want to save tonight and that's why I'm writing to you.

I know that tonight is one of the very rare times in a person's life that is nearly perfect.

Mostly life is so far from perfect that these times are our glimpses of heaven and all God's promises.

I'll see you tomorrow.

Mum.

Mary-Agnes's birth was the first time I came face to face with the bastard that is postnatal depression. If I hadn't been through childbirth before, I might not have recognised what it was, but even in hospital I sensed something was wrong with me.

After every baby, there was a magical moment in time for me, and I think it's true with most mothers and their newborns. It usually happened in the middle of the first or second night. You're breastfeeding your newborn and they're staring right into you and it feels like there's no one else in the universe but you and your baby. It's actually an ecstatic physical rush and that's when you fall in love. I waited and waited for days for that feeling with Mary-Agnes, but it never came.

What really frightened me, though, was what was going on in my head, and this is very difficult to explain. I had the most morbid thoughts imaginable. A nurse would come into my hospital room and I would imagine her corpse. I saw corpses of just about everyone, even my new baby. I had an obsession with mortality.

On the morning I left the hospital, one of the nurses left a postnatal depression booklet on the end of my bed. I hadn't said anything to anyone about the images in my head, but after I read that booklet, I managed to convince myself that the symptoms it described didn't have anything to do with me. And in a way, that was true. I didn't feel particularly depressed.

I could smile at visitors and chat normally, and I loved holding the baby and snuggling into her.

I went home and for the first few weeks nothing got any worse. But nothing got any better either. I functioned quite well, and I loved Mary-Agnes, but there was an invisible wall between me and everything else, and my morbid thoughts continued.

The mornings were the worst. I would wake up and slowly be overcome with a feeling of dread. It would start in the pit of my stomach and then crawl its way through the rest of me. It was the same feeling as waking up and then remembering something terrible had happened the day before. The problem was that nothing terrible had happened, but I felt something would. My foremost thought, day in and day out, was that we were all going to die.

Mary-Agnes developed reflux after a couple of weeks at home and she screamed for most of the day. She was the first baby I'd had that I couldn't settle, and I nearly lost my mind with tiredness. The only thing that would temporarily soothe her was the sound of the vacuum cleaner. I used to turn it on and put it next to her cot, and that would give me about twenty minutes of peace. I blew two vacuum motors before she was three months old.

One thing I was determined to succeed at was breastfeeding. Before Mary-Agnes, I used to joke that I breastfed all of my kids for four months – if you add it up – and that was pretty much the case. I went through three or four bouts of mastitis during that first year with Mary-Agnes. Nothing was going to stop me from breastfeeding her. Not even swollen, burning, infected breasts.

So, we all plodded along, the baby screamed from morning till night, and the mother was a nutcase who thought about death all day. The kids kept going to school and Chris kept leaving for work early in the morning and eating his ham-and-cheese sandwich for lunch. Then one day the camel's back was broken by a very unlikely straw.

I was feeding Mary-Agnes on the couch in the lounge room and saw a newsflash come up on the telly – something about Princess Diana having possibly broken her leg in a car accident. I shushed everyone and didn't get off that couch again for the rest of the day. I'd been obsessed with the dramas since Diana's Martin Bashir interview in which she dished on her relationship with Prince Charles and said, 'There were three of us in this marriage,' referring to her husband's mistress, Camilla Parker-Bowles. When the interview aired in 1995, I'd hosted a champagne brunch for all my girlfriends and we crammed onto my couch to watch it together, intermittently yelling at the kids to be quiet. I was sitting on the same couch nursing baby Mary-Agnes when the news came in that Princess Diana was dead. I could barely breathe.

In my head, of course, I was convinced that my morbid merry-go-round finally had a point to it. We *were* all dying, and what better proof of that than this cherished woman being crushed to death in a tunnel?

Chris walked into the kitchen later that night to find me on the floor, sobbing my heart out. I hadn't told him anything of what had been happening in my head, and he was more than a bit confused to see me bawling my eyes out in the corner.

He stood there for a while, before asking me, 'And ... you're sure ... you're ... you're sure you're just crying about Princess Diana?'

I made an appointment to see a doctor the next day, and within twenty-four hours I was taking the antidepressant Aropax. Within a week, whatever part of my brain that had gone on holiday was back at work and life was nearly normal again. My doctor said the Aropax wouldn't give me a high, it would just make me who I was supposed to be. I still disagree with that predication. I was never that nice. For the six months that I took antidepressants I was an absolute delight to be around. I think Chris decided to make hay while the sun shone; I didn't bat an eyelid when he brought visiting dentists home for dinner, and I think I even told him he should go to the pub more often for a couple of beers after work.

I don't think it was all the drug's doing, though. I was deliriously happy to be well again, and Mary-Agnes became the focus of my world. She still cried an awful lot, but something in me changed. I had always expected my babies to sleep through the night and have at least a two-hour afternoon nap. Mary-Agnes simply didn't want to fit into this age-old plan, and I decided to throw away the rule book and take my lead from her.

So, lucky Mary-Agnes had a glorious bohemian infancy by me accidentally 'attachment parenting' her. She breastfed when and where she wanted until she was nearly two, and slept in my bed until she was seven.

That desperate day in 2013, Mary-Agnes knew something was wrong with me and she knew I was in a hotel on Commercial Road. Apparently I had sent her a text message saying as much, but I have no recollection of doing so. Mary-Agnes left school (she was sixteen at the time) and went hotel-hopping. She wasn't going to stop until she found me.

When she got to the Hotel Saville, she asked the staff at the reception desk if they had a booking under my name. They didn't. Then she described what I looked like and asked if anyone matching my description had booked in. That's when I imagine the hotel called the ambulance. In my version of events, the receptionist doesn't let Mary-Agnes into my room. The reality is different. I try not to think about my sixteen-year-old daughter seeing my lifeless body carted away on a stretcher.

Waking up in hospital after trying to end your life is horrendous. Especially waking up realising benzodiazepines can't kill you. What an idiot. If you're lucky, you land in a hospital bed, not a morgue, after a suicide attempt. Of course, a part of me was relieved I'd failed. I'd survived. But the task of putting myself together felt enormous. Seeing the look of worry, disappointment, anger and hurt on my loved ones' faces killed me more than the bloody benzodiazepines ever would. If only they knew how bewildered I was.

There's a fine line you have to walk after trying to kill yourself because of your alcoholism. You can't mope around, because you need to get on with things and return to the living, but you also can't look like you don't give a shit about what everyone's just been through because of you. And while you're walking that tightrope, you also need to avoid any temptation to drink again.

I'm glad it didn't end that day in that shitty hotel, which has since been renovated by *The Block* and sold off as million-dollar apartments. I certainly don't have another one in me. I couldn't put myself or my family through another suicide attempt, no matter what the future holds. I've done enough damage. I don't know that I've come to terms with the pain I've caused, but I know for now, for me, suicide would be a karmic crime, if nothing else. And nowadays I live by a quote from my grandmother, 'It's a great life if you don't weaken.'

*

I was sent to the Albert Road Clinic, a psychiatric hospital. It would be the first of many visits. I had my own room and the nineties décor was comfortingly familiar. There were no TVs in the rooms. My psychiatrist was a kind and softly spoken man. Even though the clinic was a community full of people with mental-health issues, it was still a community and I got very involved. I became close with the other patients and invested in their recovery. It's an intimate thing to meet someone when they're at their weakest and most vulnerable.

In group therapy, you get to know people inside out and back to front. Surrounded by suicidal alcoholics, drug addicts and anorexics, I felt myself coming back to life.

I met the most beautiful girl at Albert Road. Her name was Katie and she would have been in her twenties. She was a chronic alcoholic like me. Towards the end of my stay, Katie's doctor told her there was nothing more he could do for her. She was going to die. Her liver and her body were shutting down in front of us. Still, she couldn't resist the urge. The monster inside her was stronger than her will to live. The doctor told her he couldn't see her anymore because he couldn't watch her die. So, she left.

I saw Katie the morning of her departure, and she told me she was going to drink as soon as she got out. She said, 'There's nothing I can do to stop it. I have to have it. No one knows how terrified I am.' I knew how terrified she was. She was going to drink to stop the terror, like I had done so many times.

Years later I did a show at the Melbourne Arts Centre and at the end of it, I signed autographs in the foyer. I looked up and I saw Katie. She was crying, but she looked amazing. I'd spoken about addiction in my show and she hugged me and told me she was sober. It was like hugging a ghost. She was alive, and sober, and well. She should have been dead, but she wasn't. I was in total awe and held her tightly. I wanted to ask her how she did it, but she slipped away in the crowd. I don't know where she is now.

After leaving the Albert Road Clinic, I kept going to weekly recovery meetings. I was having a smoke out the front of the building one day before the meeting started, when a bloke I didn't recognise came up to me. 'Good to see you're alive,' he said. 'The last time I saw you, you were in a really bad way.'

I looked at him quizzically, racking my brain for a sliver of memory.

'I had to put you in a taxi, you couldn't stand up straight. I bought you a toothbrush from 7-Eleven and gave you $50 to get home safe.'

I started to apologise and offer to pay him back, but he cut me off.

'Nah, I'm only kidding. I'm an alcoholic too and I've never seen you before,' he cracked. I laughed so much I cried.

Another day, I sat across from a long-term prisoner who was allowed to leave jail to come to recovery meetings. He didn't look particularly scary or menacing to me, until he shared his story. He was given a life sentence for a violent, heinous murder.

He had come to terms with spending the rest of his life behind bars in jail. 'I'm a narcissistic sociopath and an alcoholic, and I accept that the only place for me is a jail cell. I need to be locked up,' he told the group. It was extraordinary to see the power of recovery, to see a murderer own his deep flaws and accept his punishment for them. I guess, self-awareness is a side effect of the treatment.

Since then, when I start obsessing over my mistakes and stabbing myself with pangs of guilt, I remind myself that I haven't killed anyone. I'm not a narcissistic sociopath serving life for murder. I'm just a boring, run-of-the-mill alcoholic.

*

Two days after I got out of the Albert Road Clinic, I was back on stage. I worked my ringer off for the next year. I lived off 20 per cent of my earnings and poured the rest into my tax bill. Somehow, I managed to pay it off in twelve months. No longer in debt, I was thrilled that any money I made from then on was mine. For Christmas in 2013, I booked a beach shack on the Yorke Peninsula for me and the kids. They were so excited. It was a wonderful place and it meant the kids could spend the summer with their cousins and grandparents, who were all nearby. It was expensive, but I figured we deserved it. If I was going to be in the land of the living, I may as well live.

Almost immediately after I booked the beach shack, my new management team informed me that someone was claiming I owed them $20 000 for unpaid services. I asked for receipts; they didn't have any. They said I'd signed off on the fees when I was drunk. That's what happens when you're an alcoholic – people take advantage of you. They can blame everything on the booze and get away with it.

In 2010, I performed a hit season of my show *On a Wing and a Prayer* at the Sydney, Melbourne and Adelaide comedy festivals. I sold a substantial number of tickets and, of that, I got paid less than 10 per cent of the sales. Another year, I was told I hadn't turned a profit at the Melbourne International Comedy Festival, despite having packed crowds in the audience. Even though I turned up to work every night and did my job, I wouldn't be getting a paycheque for the festival. Imagine doing a shift at McDonald's, serving cheeseburgers to a restaurant full of customers, only to find out you wouldn't be paid because the expenses outweighed the profit that night and others were getting a 50 per cent cut. It's ludicrous. I'm sure my audience would have been furious to find out their ticket price had been supporting everyone except me and my family.

When I found out I hadn't made a profit that year, I was shattered. I remember running into a woman who worked backstage at the Melbourne International Comedy Festival after a show. She touched my arm sympathetically and said, 'I get so angry watching how hard you work.' I didn't feel anger, only shame. I was still suffering from a severe case of imposter syndrome, inflamed by my belief that I was the Lance Armstrong of the comedy world because I couldn't perform without a drink, so part of me felt like I didn't deserve my share of the profits. It's hard to stick up for yourself and ask to be paid what you're worth when you believe you're worthless and feel silenced with self-loathing. Even harder when you're a woman. And almost impossible when you're an alcoholic.

After finally finding the strength to put things right, it felt like I still couldn't escape. My new management in 2013 wanted the 'outstanding invoice' matter dealt with before the end of the year, so they gave me access to their lawyer and in the end I had to take a deal, which wiped me out financially. I had to ask my mum, a pensioner, to pay for the beach shack. I've only just paid her back. It was suffocating to feel like I had no control of my finances despite working so hard to make a difference. When I was married, the traditional ideals meant Chris held the coin pocket, and all these years later it seemed almost nothing had changed. I still wasn't in control. But it was even worse because now, it seemed to me, too many didn't have my best interests at heart. The same shit, different bucket. No matter how hard I tried to get ahead, my past kept holding me back. I thought about the one line of Shakespeare that stuck in my brain at boarding school, 'I am in blood stepp'd in so far that, should I wade no more, returning were as tedious as go o'er.'

CHAPTER 6

A DIRE WARNING

DOGS BARK. AFTER MY FAILED SUICIDE ATTEMPT and stint at the Albert Road Clinic, I managed to go twelve months without relapsing. The ABC had approached me to do an *Australian Story* episode, and I knew I couldn't lie to the entire country (again), pretending to be sober when I wasn't. And so, I white-knuckled it so I could say in all honesty that I hadn't had a drink in a year. The episode aired in September 2014 and they titled it 'The Pursuit of Happiness'.

My friend and fellow comic Eddie Perfect introduced the program by saying, 'Fiona is a fearlessly courageous comedian: a real truth teller. She sees truth as being like that burning pot on the stove that you just can't help but pick up with your bare hands, even though you know it's going to hurt. She's so courageous on stage, confronting some of her own personal demons very publicly, as you'll see in tonight's program. So this is her story. It's been a tough road but she has just achieved her first year in recovery, and is back performing to sell-out audiences. She's also returned to Alice and the family home she abandoned three years ago at the height of her problems.'

Visiting the house for the first time since I packed my carry-on suitcase bound for Melbourne and vowing to never come back was emotional. It was like stepping into an old pair of shoes with familiar, well-worn soles and remembering the painful blisters they gave you wearing them in. I burst into heavy tears looking at the photos on the mantle. They were snapshots of a happier time, before everything changed so much. Nobody was home except for the dog. The land of do as you please was abnormally quiet. Speaking to the camera after my visit, I said, 'I was very impressed by how tidy the house was. And it does have Chris's mark on it now and it isn't my house. And I'm really okay with that. I don't think I could have stayed. I know now, seeing the house.'

My parents, sister Cate, daughter Tess and friends Lawrence Mooney and Paul McDermott were all interviewed for the show, which largely focused on my alcoholism. I wasn't at all daunted at the thought of speaking about my disease, once again, and I was pretty interested to hear my family and friends' recollections of my life. Lawrence had seen me at my darkest and drunkest. On the episode, he said, 'When you're that drunk that it's showing up on stage and you're collapsing, you know, not turning up to gigs or being on shows pissed, that's just going to end up in a car crash. At the beginning of last year when Fiona was hospitalised and her, you know, life was in danger, there was a cloak that gathered around her very quickly. I went to visit her and she was, um … she was very alone.'

I'd certainly come a long way in a year. The episode ended with me saying, 'I don't hope so much to be an inspiration, but I do hope I'm a dire warning. And if you are an alcoholic: the reason we need to clean up our act is because we really do make life nearly unbearable for our loved ones. I've had far too many shoulders that I could lean on than a girl deserves, but I'm so grateful.'

It was true, at the time. But I can't watch the episode now, knowing what was to come. I saw a beer coaster once that said, 'Well, apparently rock bottom has a basement.' I was about to fall down the stairs into said basement, bruising my left side on impact.

Not long after *Australian Story*, I was on my way to see my psychiatrist, still feeling pretty chuffed with myself for not drinking. Travelling past the Prince Alfred Hospital on the tram, I smugly thought, *I haven't been there in a while.* As I was flipping the hospital the bird in my mind, the tram screamed to a halt to avoid hitting a motorcycle on the tracks. It was a new tram, so the floor was shiny and slippery. I slid headfirst through the middle of the carriage like a bullet; I was wearing a fluffy jacket and must have looked like a flying fuzzy-wuzzy cleaning cloth. I remember the sound of screams as my head hit the corner of the tram driver's box with force. I was knocked out cold and came to with a doctor standing above me. He said, 'I work at the Prince Alfred, we need to take you to hospital to get your head checked out.'

'No way, I'm not going there, not today. I've gone so long. I'm an alcoholic,' I pleaded, with an enormous egg growing on my head. I don't know why I felt the need to tell him I was an alcoholic.

Once inside the hospital, I messaged Biddy, and she rushed to my side. She pulled back the curtain to my cubicle, sat down next to my bed and asked me, 'Are you okay?' I told her what had happened and that I was all right. She looked at me and said, 'Oh my God, you're not drunk.' She was so used to seeing me in hospital for alcohol-induced issues, she was shocked.

Even though my injury had nothing to do with booze, it was another wake-up call. They did a CAT scan of my brain at the hospital and discovered a mild brain injury. It was a direct result of my drinking. I'd done damage to my frontal lobe, which is the planning and memory part of the brain. I've always been forgetful – when I moved to Alice Springs I left my suitcase with my life's savings of $1500 in the middle of Franklin Street in Adelaide; I lost my passport and boarding ticket at Kuala Lumpur airport on my way back from the Edinburgh Festival Fringe; and once I even lost a kid at the bottle shop – so another knock to my memory was the last thing I needed.

My friend Jasmin understood my pathological propensity to lose things. On one of her visits to our place in Alice Springs, I was searching high and low for Henry's birth certificate. He was in a foul mood because I'd lost it and stormed out of the living room, slamming the door behind him. I heard Biddy ask nobody in particular, 'Why doesn't Mum ever know where anything is?'

Jasmin explained it to her: 'Biddy, there's a part of everybody's brain that tells them where their car keys are and whose birthday it is next and what time they're supposed to be somewhere, and your Mum just can't use that part of her brain.'

'But why?'

'Because that's where she keeps all of her favourite lines from *The Young Ones*, the theme songs from American sitcoms and Earl Spencer's speech from Princess Di's funeral.'

The doctor at the hospital didn't explain my problem to me quite so eloquently, but she assured me that it wouldn't get worse. Over time, it could even get better.

*

A matter of weeks after my *Australian Story* and tram incident, I unclenched my fists and stopped white-knuckling. I told myself a year was a solid effort and I deserved a drink. Returning to my addiction was heinous. Being awake and upright was torturous for me, so I gave myself a four-hour window in which I could disappear. From 11 am to 3 pm, I could do whatever I needed to get through the day before Mary-Agnes got home from school. One day I caught up with a girl in my recovery group and she gave me the number for her dealer. I now had access to cocaine and used it at least twice a week.

I usually instigated my own relapses by having heated words with someone. I see now that sick pervasive logic. I did my best to extract an insult from Chris or my sisters. Insults are like drink vouchers to an alcoholic.

Up until this point, I'd only ever done cocaine recreationally, a bump at a party or a line in a bathroom stall after a gig. I remember walking the streets of Kings Cross in Sydney looking for pills at sunrise, but I never got addicted to drugs in the same way I was addicted to alcohol. Cocaine gave me a nice buzz, but it didn't numb the pain like vodka. Plus, it clogged up my nostrils and made me sniff a suspicious amount. I had a gorgeous ragdoll cat in Melbourne called Mrs Fooks and I pretended to be allergic to her to cover up my persistent sniffing. No one has a cold all year long.

I only ever did one show high on coke. It was a gig at the Harold Park Hotel in Sydney. I was on fire. I understood why Robin Williams was one of the best in the business; coke makes you funnier, braver, totally uninhibited. The audience gave me a standing ovation and I realised I could never do cocaine before a show again for fear of falling into old rabbit-foot talisman habits.

One day, Biddy, who was living in Melbourne at the time, found a baggie under my pillow and showed Mary-Agnes, dramatically telling her, 'Mum's gone, Mary, she'll never come back from this.' I'd just purchased an expensive formal dress for Mary-Agnes when she brought up the discovery. I can't remember if she waved the bag of white powder in my face or if I planted that memory for dramatic effect. I do remember exactly what she said to me, though: 'I don't want things; I just want a mother.'

I'm ashamed that I expected my older children to automatically be in cahoots with me when it came to protecting Mary-Agnes. Where were my morals to be angry at one child for telling another about my drug use? Lack of insight and desperate narcissism were side effects of this three-pronged disease of the body, mind and soul. My alcohol and drug use no longer offered me relief like it once had. My truth at the time was that I would die if I didn't drink or use.

By the end of 2014, I knew I was failing Mary-Agnes as a mother, but I was too scared or weak or stubborn to admit it. Henry had to say the words for me. He rang with concern in his voice, to tell me he was worried that if I didn't get my act together, Mary-Agnes would be taken away by the Family and Community Services department. Imagine trying to find the words to say, 'Mum, you need to get your act together or Family Services could take Mary away from you.' I felt so sad for the young man who had to do that. I was proud of Henry and so deeply ashamed. But mostly I just felt spent.

As usual, Henry was right. Mary-Agnes was starting Year 12 and she deserved better. She needed stability, not a mother hiding baggies under her pillow. I had to give her up, as much as it hurt. It was decided that Mary-Agnes would live with the family of one of her friends from school. She gradually moved all of her clothes to their house, but she still dropped into my place as she pleased. They were a lovely family who adored Mary-Agnes and, by all accounts, it was the best thing for her. She blitzed Year 12 and I will be forever grateful to the family who looked after my daughter when I couldn't.

My apartment was eerily quiet without Mary-Agnes. Because I didn't have to put on a fake happy face anymore, I was free to blow my life up. My four-hour window from 11 am to 3 pm was extended and I did whatever I had to do to get through my waking hours. I spent several thousand dollars on cocaine during that lonely time, but I tried my best to steer clear of my poison of choice: Smirnoff. I was seriously worried about my liver, so I justified my coke habit by telling myself it was the healthy choice.

It was around this time that I had another incident on a Brisbane stage. You'd think I would have learned my lesson after the 2009 fiasco but, alas, I hadn't. I caught a plane from Melbourne to Brisbane for a couple of corporate gigs. I was coked up to my eyeballs when the comedy booker picked me up from the airport in his sports car. I could feel myself coming down before the gig, so I messaged my friend Michael who had introduced himself to me on Facebook as a fan years earlier and had become a trusted confidant and warm place to crash in Brisbane. He was a gay man with a bit of a party boy reputation, and not a single judgemental bone in his body, which I appreciated. Plus, we had the exact same taste in trashy television. I told Michael I needed a hit, and he understood. I was aching for 'medicine' to keep the withdrawals at bay. Michael met me at my hotel room and we racked up together. I told him if the comedy booker walked in, he had to pretend he was from AA and we were praying. It was insane, I was insane.

At the gig, a comic I knew asked me how I was, and I replied, 'Pretty fucked, actually.' I knew I couldn't have a drink because the booker was watching me, so the comic offered me a pre-show joint. As soon as I inhaled, I knew I'd made a mistake. I was used to performing inebriated, but not high. When I got on stage, in front of an audience of three hundred, I froze. I opened my mouth, but no words came out. The venue was deathly silent. I whispered, 'Can somebody please help me? I think I'm having a nervous breakdown.' I felt three hundred pairs of eyes on me, but no one moved. I can't remember how I eventually got off the stage, but I know Michael came to get me and took me back to his house. He scooped me up like an injured little bird that'd just flown into a window. At his place, I tossed and turned until the early hours of the morning, hallucinating that the three hundred people from the show were outside my door demanding their money back. Michael kept the horrors at bay, and over the next four days, he took care of me. We watched *The Real Housewives* together and I slowly recovered from the shame and humiliation, like a stunned little bird healing in a shoe box.

CHAPTER 7

MY BEATING
HEART

M Y DAUGHTERS TESS AND MARY-AGNES FOUND ME
in the attic, stark naked and screaming at the
top of my lungs. By the time an ambulance arrived, I was
unconscious. They all thought it was another suicide attempt.
The place looked like a crime scene. There was an empty packet
of Panadeine Forte on the floor and a full bottle of Valium
nearby. It wouldn't have been full if I had tried to kill myself.
And I would never choose to go out by paracetamol poisoning.
With my nursing background, I knew that overdosing on
paracetamol would destroy my organs and if I didn't make a

good job of it, I could end up on dialysis for the rest of my life. It's the last method I would use. We may never know what led to my two-and-a-half week coma, but I have a theory …

I have little to no memory of the month leading up to the coma. At the time, I thought I was developing early Alzheimer's disease. I was forgetting things, important things, like my kids' names. I know I was scheduled to appear on the reality TV series *I'm a Celebrity … Get Me Out of Here!* on Channel 10 and had gotten all my shots for South Africa. That's as close as I got to Kruger National Park in 2015. The week before the coma, I also went to a photo shoot for an upcoming comedy webseries, but I only know that because there's a photo of it. Duh. In the image, I look sickly. My skin is yellow, my eyes are sunken and my shoulders are hunched over as though I don't have the strength to sit up straight. It was a hauntingly scary hint of what was to come.

The morning of the coma, I had a molar pulled at the dentist. The extraction went on and on; the tooth fell apart and the dentist almost had to put his knee on my chest to yank it all out. Walking down Commercial Road on my way home with a gaping hole in my mouth and the taste of dried blood on my tongue, I remember feeling desperately sad. It was the second tooth I had to have removed in two years and I knew it was the result of being self-employed, an alcoholic and the financial fallout from both. What broke my heart the most was that my (ex)husband was a dental technician and he had a share in a dental surgery. And yet, there I was, with a mouth full of needy teeth and a serious dent in my bank account.

It was 2015 and I'd never felt so spent in my life. I thought, *How will I ever go on?* I must have stopped by a pharmacy and picked up the Panadeine Forte the dentist had prescribed for the pain, but I don't remember doing so. I can understand why everyone thought I'd tried to commit suicide: I had form, I was a relapsed alcoholic and my demons were in full force. But as I mentioned earlier, paracetamol poisoning wasn't my style.

When I arrived at the Austin Hospital, the doctor told my family, 'Her injuries are catastrophic, and we simply cannot give you any false hope that she will survive the night.'

My sister Cate collapsed into the arms of her eldest son, my nephew Ned. He held her for dear life as she asked the unspoken question on everyone's behalf. 'If she doesn't die tonight, is there any chance she will wake up?'

The answer was a shake of the head and an 'I'm sorry' from the medical man. *Not a chance in hell,* was what he couldn't say.

When I did miraculously survive the night, the doctors gave me a 14 per cent chance of survival, and a 7 per cent chance of waking up normal, without brain damage. My organs were in almost total failure. By that stage, Chris had arrived from Alice Springs. He sat in the hospital hallway and cried openly, 'She's still my wife.'

The girls, especially Mary-Agnes, were desperate for my friend Jasmin to arrive and put them at ease, in the gentle, generous way she always did. She would know exactly what to do in this situation and just how to reassure them that I was going to be okay. When she arrived and saw me in the hospital bed hooked up to the machines with tubes coming out of my mouth, she couldn't see my 'aura'. She thought the worst. Shielding my kids from the horror she felt, she stepped outside for a moment. I can't begin to imagine how hard it was for all of them to see me like that – especially thinking it was another suicide attempt. Part of them must have considered it might be for the best. If I died, at least I would be out of my misery, I would be released from my alcoholism and my desperation.

I don't think anyone really expected me to wake up. But I did. I was still very unwell when I regained consciousness after fifteen days in the coma. I remember being in excruciating pain. It felt like every part of my body was on fire and the only touch that soothed me was Tess. I can still feel her beautiful, safe hands comforting me. When she held my hand, I knew I had a home somewhere in her.

Tess had told everyone, 'No one is to ever make her feel guilty about this.' But I did.

Worse than the pain was the look on people's faces when they came into my room, a mask of shame and stigma. Everyone thought I had tried to kill myself, but no one would say it out loud. Some words are safer left unspoken. The nurse in charge of the ward mustn't have got the memo, though. She bluntly asked me, 'Why did you do what you did?' I was too weak to explain or defend myself. Or to tell her to rack off.

Waking up was exhausting. Every time I opened my eyes, it was like rising from the coma all over again. I had to remember where I was and what I had been through, over and over. Plus, I looked like Laa-Laa from the Teletubbies. Because of my liver failure, my skin was bright yellow and I was horrendously bloated. I kept saying to the nurses, 'I don't look like this. I don't know what's wrong. This isn't me.' They eventually took me downstairs to a surgical room and drained two-and-a-half litres of fluid out of me in one sitting. It took weeks for the rest of the fluid to disappear. When it did, I was a tiny 50 kilograms.

When people asked me what it felt like being in a coma, I struggled to find the words. I'm still trying to make sense of what I saw while I was at the gates of the afterlife. It's a sight I will never forget, one that simultaneously frightened and awed me. Maybe it was nothing more than a dream fuelled by a cocktail of lifesaving drugs and my rebooting mind, but it felt real to me. I saw my broken heart. I couldn't take my eyes off it. It was like a bruise days after the injury, turning dark purple, then black before ripening to a painful yellow. My broken but still-beating heart was impressive. It looked like it had one massive gunshot wound on the left upper half, and another just under it, not as big but bleeding profusely. Was my coma trying to tell me I needed to mend my broken heart? Or was I hallucinating on morphine? I'll never know.

*

Three days out of the coma, I noticed my sisters Emily and Cate were talking into their wrists. Emily was saying, 'Yeah, she's alive. They think she's going to be okay,' holding her wrist to her mouth.

And Cate was saying, 'Yeah, she's in ICU, she's awake. She doesn't look great.'

I confusedly asked them, 'What are you doing?'

'Oh, it's the new Samsung microchip in our wrists, we've all got them. You do know you've been in a coma for seven years?' I just about lost my mind.

Later, on stage, I would repeat all of it word for word. I returned the serve that night when Emily and Dad were keeping vigil. Everyone was especially on the lookout for brain damage. Dad patted my hand as he rose to stretch his legs and asked me if there was anything he could bring back for me. I said no but thank you, and then waited until he left to turn to Emily and say with a straight face, 'I have absolutely no idea who that man is!'

Speaking to Mary-Agnes, I put pieces of memory together to form my theory. Every time she stayed with me during that period, she would say, 'Mum, you really need to get that heater fixed. I always feel so sleepy when I'm here.' In fact, when I first got the keys to the apartment, I asked the real-estate agent if the heater was safe. He said, 'They're the safest gas heaters on the market.' They didn't test my blood for carbon-monoxide poisoning, but I'm certain that's what happened to me. It's known as the 'silent killer' because the gas is colourless and odourless, so it can incapacitate humans without them realising it. Prolonged exposure can cause brain damage and death.

I've come to understand that it really doesn't matter what specifically caused my organ failure and resulting coma. It was a consequence of being in active addiction and it was a collision course that had been set in motion many years before. Having survived the coma, there were still some frightening times ahead. At one stage I had a perilously low white blood cell count and I was reminded by staff that I wasn't out of the woods yet.

I feel as though I was protected somehow during that time and in a way the coma itself actually saved my life. I haemorrhaged spectacularly from an undiagnosed duodenal ulcer while I was in intensive care. If that had happened at home and under the influence, I probably would have bled to death. My physical recovery was painstaking. I had picked up a staph infection. Eating was virtually impossible. I would often bite into my tongue, while I was out to it. For many months my tongue felt like a swollen block of sandpaper.

There were special moments too. My cousin and childhood friend Eugene dropped in most nights to give me a lift. My friend Mary-Anne was on hand for help in the shower, playing cards or just a good gossip and lots of laughs.

I returned to the Albert Road Clinic for three months to recover physically and mentally. When I arrived, I was very frail.

My bloating had settled, but I still glowed yellow from liver failure. The staff were worried about having me there because it's not a medical hospital. Two days after I was admitted, I was standing at the nurses' station when my psychiatrist put his hand on my shoulder and asked, 'Have you eaten?'

Those three words triggered a tsunami of tears. In as long as I could remember before the coma, I hadn't experienced anything as humane and caring as that simple gesture and that question. When I started crying, I couldn't stop. His hand on my shoulder opened the flood gates. I think I cried for six weeks straight. I was crying for myself, for my life before and what was to come in the life ahead of me.

I was desperately homesick, but for what? My flat had been packed up and my belongings put in storage while I was in hospital, presumed nearly dead. I would cry like a little kid, 'I want to go home, I want to go home,' rocking back and forth. Then I'd say to myself, 'You don't have a home, you idiot.' It was brutal.

At the clinic, I had to relearn how to be. It was glaringly obvious that my life didn't work. I felt like I was at the end of a really long Monopoly game that I just couldn't win. I was constantly being sent to jail. Do not pass Go. Do not collect $200. I was so bored of myself and my behaviours, occasional cocaine and frequent vodka relapses. Being a struggling alcoholic was a real snooze fest.

Mary-Agnes visited me near daily at that time. I would marvel at this extraordinary child. In her final year of school and living away from home with her mother in a Psych ward. Lying next to me, as she always did, she told me one day, 'You know, Mum, when you were dying, I kept thinking, this isn't how it ends. I knew this had a happy ending.' The crazy thing was that I believed it too.

Mary-Agnes wrote a poem a month after the coma, and I'll have it in my phone for all time ...

First comes the phone call
The one you've always feared
'Get to the hospital'
And your ear feels like it's seared
You feel your knees tremble
You can hear your own heart
You just want to reassemble
The life that fell apart
Not knowing where to sit
Not knowing what to do
This very well may be it

For a woman you love more than you

This isn't like any other time

This time is for real

The doctors are sitting us all down

You wonder, how long will it take to heal?

You enter premature grief

You long for a mother's embrace

All they tell you is that she's sick

'This is a critical case'

You say your goodbyes

You sing her a song

You can't bear to open your eyes

To see what is wrong

But her hand you hold

And you hold it well

You remember her beautiful soul

And the stories she would tell

From within, you can find

A mere sense of peace

You tell her you'll be fine

So she can relax, at least

Together comes a family

Torn apart by rotten things

But here they sit wearily
Re-wearing old wedding rings
Whilst lying in that hospital bed
Being kept alive by machines
She went on a journey in her head
A journey in her dreams
She travelled down a country lane
And came to a fork in the road
She was then given the option
Of which way to go
Both sides led to beautiful worlds
Where birds sang and the sun shone
But the difference between the two
Was in one, she was gone
She decided to live
And that she shall do
Not in guilt and not in shame
But in happiness that is well overdue

*

My counsellor at the Albert Road Clinic was a beautiful woman named Hannah. She wasn't an alcoholic, but she got it. She was one of the few non-alcoholics who knew everything you could know about the hideous beast that is this disease. During my regular stints at the clinic over the years, Hannah and I had many one-on-ones. This time, I could hear the common sense in her words, but there was a huge chasm between what she was saying and me making it a reality. I had every resolve not to drink again, but I still didn't have control over the monster inside. Before I was discharged, Hannah and my psychiatrist held a meeting in my room. They said, 'You've taken this as far as you can take it. You came as close as you can to dying. What is your plan?' We all just stared at each other. None of us had an answer.

I went to stay with my cousin Meg in Adelaide. My first cousins have been one of the greatest joys of my life, and I knew it would be softer for me at Meg's. She was the daughter of my Uncle Maurice and Aunty Shirley, who both died too young in their forties, leaving five kids behind. It's almost with a sense of shame that I think back over everything. It was so unfair that Meg and her siblings copped so much grief and were left to fend for themselves while our family sailed merrily on with parents at the helm. And here I was, standing at Meg's door with my tail between my legs and nowhere else to go, asking her to look after me. If anyone had the right to break down, it was her, not me.

Within days of being at Meg's place, I ended up in her bathtub filled to the brim, fully clothed in jeans, boots and a jumper. I was blind drunk. I don't remember what precipitated my bath, but I knew I had selfishly crumbled and turned to my old mate alcohol. I was beyond embarrassed, but Meg was so kind. I'd drunk all of her husband's red wine, and Meg told me she was thrilled about it because they were separating and they still hadn't divvied up the cellar collection. I'd made a hell of a dent. I was admitted back into a psychiatric clinic in Adelaide. If I thought what I'd been through up until this point was rough, I had no idea what was to come.

When I was released from my second psych ward in as many months, I went to stay with my sister Genevieve, in her small two-bedroom flat. She obviously still had a lot of issues with me and was justifiably angry. The air was thick with tension and one night she yelled at me, 'That coma didn't just happen, you know!' I knew I'd treated her badly and maybe she didn't really want me there, but I had nowhere else to go. I just tried to make myself as small as possible. I was like a lamb, scuttling into my room, avoiding eye contact and arguments like the slaughterhouse.

Genevieve is a teacher and left for work early in the morning. I slept in until 11 am to avoid seeing her at the breakfast table. When I eventually rose from bed, I would scrounge around the house and my handbag for money and head to the bottle shop wearing a disguise to buy as many mini bottles of vodka as I could afford when I was as poor as a church mouse. I spent the day trying to disappear in a vodka haze. I made sure I stopped drinking and started white-knuckling in the early afternoon so I wouldn't be drunk when Genevieve got home. I went to bed early.

*

My first corporate gig post the coma was in Sydney. I caught a taxi from Genevieve's flat to the airport. I was a bundle of nerves, but the gig went well. I was still revelling in being able to perform without my pre-show ritual. Even though I still wasn't free from addiction in my life, I was completely free of it in my career. I no longer felt like the Lance Armstrong of the comedy world. I wasn't a drug cheat anymore. I could make people laugh even when I was stone-cold sober. It was one of the only pockets of joy in my life at that time.

I was punching out incredible stand-up material about the coma, but I was still living it in real life. On stage, I would say, 'People ask me how I write my shows and I say, I don't. I wait. How lucky was that coma! You can't buy material like that.' In real life, there was nothing lucky about it.

On stage, I would say, 'I actually woke up weird after the coma. For three days I was in a really vile mood, I was just an arsehole. And my doctor explained it was because I was in organ failure and your liver is apparently your anger organ. That made sense because I woke up livid.' In real life, I still felt despicable.

On stage, I would say, 'I must have looked 101 when I woke up, and this nurse asked me, "What did you used to do?" I said, "Oh, I used to blow sailors down by the wharf during the war." "Which war?" "Both wars."' In real life, I was fighting my own cold war. And losing on both fronts. I would look out into the audience and think, *Oh God, if only you knew how broke and desperate I am.*

Making light of my near-death experience felt entirely natural. My coping mechanism has always been to laugh through pain. The stage was the only space where I could freely talk about what happened to me without judgement. I always felt safe with my audience. I owned my shit and they applauded me for it. It was emancipating.

Another corporate gig at the time meant I flew to Brisbane. I was kidding myself I was okay, but the reality was very different. The truth is, I don't remember all that much but luckily my friend Michael came to my rescue again. I wasn't answering calls from my agent and they got worried and called him and he went to check on me at the Sofitel. He left work early and it turned out he knew the guy at reception and though the man wouldn't hand over a key, he told Michael what room I was in and let him into the lift. Michael knocked and knocked and knocked and knocked and eventually I let him in. I was bawling my eyes out and could barely walk. Michael had to help me use the toilet, undress and put me to bed. I passed out. He stayed on the couch to keep an eye on me and the next day he helped me get to the airport for my flight. It wasn't the only time Michael looked after me but all the other times I can remember much more of what happened. One time I holed up at his place and binge-watched *Grace and Frankie* with him while I popped codeine tablets like Tic Tacs (his words, not mine) until I sobered up enough to go home.

CHAPTER 8

THE HEALER

B Y NOW, EVERYONE KNEW I WAS DRINKING. I WAS powerless to stop. Dogs bark even when you tell them to shut up and put the hose on them over the fence. My girlfriend Mary-Anne saw how much I needed help and she took me to meet a 'healer' who was psychic and had treated Mary-Anne's nephew who had a brain injury after a go-kart accident. I can't remember what the healer told me during my first 'reading', but I do recall feeling trapped as soon as she started to speak, as though I couldn't escape the torrent of words flying out of her mouth. About a week after our meeting, the healer told Mary-Anne, 'Your friend is in trouble. She's going to die. I've got to find her.' It was decided by Mary-Anne and the healer that I would move into the healer's house.

When I landed at Adelaide airport after a disastrous, drunken gig in Melbourne, the healer was there to pick me up and take me back to her house. I don't know how she knew where I would be, maybe she really was psychic. She was the tallest woman I'd ever seen. Her face gave nothing away. I didn't like her very much. There was a glint in her eyes I didn't trust, and her incessant talking filled me with unease. But I was so far in the depths of relapse, I didn't even question the absurdity of moving in with a total stranger.

As I said, it had all been arranged. I was going to live with the healer and follow her treatment plan, which involved detoxing by continuing to drink in limited quantities, smoke the occasional ice pipe and curb the tremors by administering Valium in small amounts (can you believe it?). It was a protocol with strict dosages, like a medical treatment plan or an episode of *the goop lab* on Netflix. The thinking behind the treatment plan was called 'the psychedelic renaissance', where psychedelic drugs are used to address hard-to-treat mental-health conditions such as PTSD, depression, anxiety and, you guessed it, addiction. The healer's protocol worked by taking meth (in small doses on rare occasions) to open the mind and deal with deep-seated issues without fear, stigma or prohibition.

There was a gathering of others the night of my arrival. A young girl and a handsome English man named Adam were living there at the time and they welcomed me with open arms and a cold beer. The healer beckoned her neighbour Sue to meet me. She'd watched my *Australian Story* episode a year earlier and had felt a connection to me. Sue had got to know the healer after she helped a family member with mental-health issues. Sue, who was once a registered nurse, seemed to intimately understand the complexities of mental illness and addiction. I felt relieved to be surrounded by people who got it, people who wouldn't look down their nose at me, people who could separate me from my disease.

Sue told me later that the healer had predicted my arrival. Weeks before I moved into the house, the healer had told Sue, 'There's a comedian who's really sick. She's going to come and live with me.'

The house was an old bungalow in Adelaide, which was the backdrop of my youth. Every street and every corner housed a memory from my teenage years at boarding school, as a Cabra girl, pining over the Sacred Heart boys. I wouldn't have stepped foot in a house like this back then.

It was the most hopeless and frightening place I'd ever seen. Maybe it was because I'd never felt so frightened or hopeless that I saw everything at that time through a lens of despair. There were between three and six people living in the house at any one time, plus people dropping by at all hours of the day and night. They were usually addicts. The house was a drug den. I paid rent, but the owner of the house seemed to be constantly chasing the healer for money. And I'm not sure the healer ever passed on my rent. Some mornings I'd wake up to her blowing smoke in my face in some kind of smoking ceremony. I'd stare at the ceiling, thinking, *What the fuck is this?*

My room was a windowless hovel. There was a double bed and a cupboard, and that's all. When I first moved in, it was messy and full of the last tenant's crap. The house had a working bee to clean it up and I remember thinking, *Who are all these young people giving a shit about my living conditions?* They were customers. I'm still haunted by the painting that hung lopsided on my wall. It was an amateur charcoal drawing of a woman leaving Earth and flying into the sun. She had a manic grin on her face and crazy eyes that were too big for the rest of her body. Hell wasn't a baby screaming for the mother it can never have; hell was this painting.

One night, the girl from across the hall called me into her room. 'I've got all of these clothes, help yourself to anything,' she said, waving at a pile of brand-new Veronika Maine and Cue outfits on her bed. They still had the tags on them and were clearly hot. It was a desperate place, full of desperate people, drug dealers, addicts and lost souls. I overheard conversations about crime and violence. I saw pain in people's eyes. I saw pain in my eyes. I tried not to look in the bathroom mirror.

When she wasn't performing smoke ceremonies on me, I had in-depth conversations with the healer about addiction. She recognised that I was addicted to two substances, alcohol and opioids. I got to know the neighbour, Sue, and we became friends. The healer gave Sue the name of an addiction specialist. I would eventually reach out to this specialist years later with Sue's help. The healer also told me about a study by a Canadian psychologist called Bruce Alexander in the 1970s that investigated whether living conditions played a role in drug addiction. When rats were placed in a small cage all alone with no friends and offered two water bottles – one filled with water and the other filled with heroin or cocaine – the rats would repetitively drink from the drug-laced bottles until they overdosed and died. But, when the rats were housed in a 'rat heaven' with friends, food, balls, wheels to play with and space to mate, the rats resisted the drug-laced water and significantly preferred the plain water. The study showed that drug addiction is as much about social and environmental factors as the drug itself. Oh, how I dreamed of escaping to my own 'rat heaven', with support, a community and nice furniture. Looking around the putrid bungalow I called home, I knew how the coked-up caged rats felt.

I survived off packages left on the doorstep by my friend Mary-Anne. No one else knew where I was; they just knew through Mary-Anne that I was alive and safe. I had cut off all contact with my family, except for sporadic phone calls with my kids. I didn't want anyone to see me in the state I was in, not to mention the place I was in. Mary-Anne would pass a hat around my sisters and friends and they'd chuck in $5 to buy me cigarettes and groceries. Some days all I had was two beers. I didn't have to function. I could sleep all day – and I did. I learned later that my bone tiredness was normal after waking up from a coma. It was a side effect that could last up to a year.

Within days of being in the house, I was horribly sick from detoxing. I couldn't walk unaided and spent my few waking hours in a horizontal position, unable to get up at all. Our neighbour Sue was asked by the healer to help me. She was conflicted because she thought I should have been in hospital, but she took it upon herself to care for me. Sue would come over every day and feed me hospital-grade Sustagen mixed with banana. At my worst, she spent days on end sitting by my bedside, only leaving to run to the loo. I was in awe of Sue's strength. At that time, she was struggling with a failing restaurant, more than enough drama in her own personal life and a backdoor neighbour called Fiona who needed her. I have no doubt that I wouldn't be alive if it weren't for Sue. Every day, she forced me to look her in the eye and told me sincerely, 'You will come back from this.'

I couldn't see how. I was incredibly spacey most of the time I was in the house. I was weak, physically and mentally. I didn't care about myself. I'd given up. I was floating above myself, as though I were watching the misery happen to someone else. I put myself somewhere else, somewhere warmer, somewhere with a window. On the few occasions I smoked meth as a part of my treatment, it was a release. A puff to escape. A puff to forget. A puff to dull the pain. But I didn't want to *not* know how sick I was. I had no interest in escaping to an alternate reality. I would dim my fear with alcohol, but I knew I needed to feel it. My life depended on it.

On my lowest days, the healer would tell me to think of my future grandkids. 'Don't you want to meet your grandchildren one day? They're coming, you need to stay alive for them,' she would say, as though she were looking into a crystal ball and could see their chubby faces. Every time I tried to picture myself holding a precious grandchild, I became emotional. Of course, I wanted to meet my hypothetical grandchildren, I just didn't know how much longer I could cling to the hope of an imaginary tiny hand wrapped around my thumb.

One morning I had a horrific anxiety attack. I couldn't breathe and the voice in my head kept repeating my mantra, 'You are so sick. You are so sick.' I asked Sue to drive me to the Royal Adelaide Hospital. I had a plan. I thought that if I could get into a psych ward and wait there safely until I could get into a long-term placement at a rehab clinic, then I would survive.

I told the nurse, 'I'm going to die out there. Can you please put me in a psych ward?' She looked at me with pity and sympathy and said, 'I'm so sorry, you're just not sick enough.' She cried. I cried. I willed myself to be sicker.

*

While I was fearing for my life, Chris's dad, Ivan, was dying. The kids were devastated – and so was I. I had a beautiful relationship with Ivan. When I was a young mother, I found him very old-school and sexist. We'd fight a lot and stir each other up. He knew exactly how to get a reaction out of me. Stirring aside, Ivan was such a good man. I don't know how he coped with the tragedies his life dealt him. He lost his wife and daughter in a plane accident; dear God, I'd forgive that man for anything.

Ivan used to come to Alice Springs for six weeks every year. I remember picking him up from the airport one day and watching him walk across the tarmac wearing a light blue shirt with khaki pants and an Akubra hat. When I spotted him, my heart burst. I was overcome with unexpected love for him. I made a decision in that moment to love him instead of fighting with him. From that day on, I did. Watching Ivan grandfather my children was perfection. He was the best grandad. He wasn't just some old guy the kids knew; he was their Papa and they adored him. He gave them his time and knew them all individually. Every birthday and every Christmas, the kids got a $25 cheque from Papa, despite the fact he was on the pension (and a real tightarse). Everything he did towards the end was for his grandkids.

I woke up on Christmas Day 2015 at 2 am and felt an outside force radiating vibrations above me. It was as though I wasn't alone anymore, help was coming, shit was going to get better. I knew instinctively that Ivan had gone. Henry called me later that morning and said, 'Papa died.' And I said, 'Yeah, I know.'

It took me ten days to get ready for the funeral, which was held in January 2016 at Our Lady of Victories Church in Glenelg, where I first saw Chris at his mother and sister's funeral all those years ago. Sue took over to get me well enough to farewell Ivan. It was like we were in training for a marathon or the Olympics. I decreased my alcohol intake to just enough to keep my hands steady and the shakes at bay. I had to use all my energy and strength to look half-human and be able to walk in a straight line.

A hair and make-up artist came over late the night before the early-morning funeral to do me up. Sitting in the make-up chair with a professional light and mirror facing me, it reminded me of the thousands of make-up chairs I'd sat in backstage at theatres and TV studios. I truly believed that part of my life was over. Never again would I sit in a make-up chair before a gig. I was going to be a homeless alcoholic forever. A Fleetwood Mac song played in the background and a single tear rolled down my cheek. I couldn't afford to ruin my make-up, so I allowed myself just one tear. Just one blink of self-pity. Just one.

In the morning, Biddy came over to help me get ready with Sue. She was the only person in my family to see the drug den. That's the beauty of Biddy, she's such a vagrant artist herself, she didn't judge me or bat an eyelid at the shithole I was living in; she'd lived in places like that all over the world. After a herculean effort, we made it. I went to Ivan's funeral. It was a perfect summer day.

I was grateful for the opportunity to grieve. It was such a release to cry for someone else. I was there inside the church, but not really. My mind was still in my windowless room in the drug den. I felt so apart from the day. I sat next to my parents halfway down the church, not with my kids in the front rows. I looked out the stained-glass windows and sobbed for them and for Ivan. I didn't go to the wake. Standing out the front of the church, with its Colloseum sandstone pillars towering above me, I asked Henry for $50 because I didn't have any money. He gave it to me, lovingly. I knew I was going to use the money to buy alcohol and drink myself stupid in my personal hell. Henry knew it too. The reality of my son handing me a $50 note from his wallet at his grandfather's funeral was a stark reminder of what I had become. I thought,

Who am I? What's happened? Where did this go so horribly wrong? Stumbling back to the drug den from the church after Ivan's funeral was the loneliest walk of my life.

*

It is strange that you can be incredibly lonely even with people around. And not every day was hideous while I was staying in what I still call the drug den. One surprising experience was a day out on a boat courtesy of Sue's friend Don. Don was a youthful 70 year old and, like many of Sue's friends and family, he went out of his way to include me in on social invitations. It was a glistening day on the water and the weather was perfection. For a fleeting moment I wondered if maybe things were going to get better starting ... now.

'You look like Liz Taylor, Fiona.' Don's compliment added to the optimism of the day.

Maybe all I needed was a new environment with new friends like Don, who didn't freak out at the sight of a glass of champagne in my hand. I recall being full of fun and laughter at the start of my nautical afternoon and I began to feel like the person I was years and years ago before all my crap started. Somebody who liked a drink and loved being where the action is. But I knew something everyone on the boat didn't. An alcoholic can't have just one. Exactly five hours later I was more Liz in *Who's Afraid of Virginia Woolf?* than the fresh-faced Liz in *Little Women*. It wasn't a good look.

Amid the bleakness, I had an unexpected ray of light. One night at the healer's house, there was a party with dancing and drinks. I must have been on something, because my memories of that night are like an abstract painting. All of a sudden across the room, I locked eyes with Pat Tohl, one of the boys who went to Sacred Heart college when I was a Cabra girl. He was stunningly handsome as a teenager, so much so that I never even bothered having a crack at him because I wasn't interested in having my heart broken (and my sister Cate pined over him). When he walked into the house, I thought I was imagining it, that he was a drug-fuelled mirage, a gorgeous Matisse painting, a dream. I couldn't understand why Pat Tohl was at a party in this place. Apparently, he'd heard through the Adelaide grapevine that I wasn't doing too well, and I was living there. We'd loosely stayed in touch since high school and both our marriages had broken down around the same time a few years earlier. We would text each other every Christmas. It was a tradition.

I had to pinch myself that night to make sure I wasn't asleep, and I pinched myself even harder when Pat and I started seeing each other. My teenage heartthrob would come over and sleep beside me every night he could. This incredibly fit and handsome bloke would curl up next to me, a tragic alcoholic living in a drug den. Every time he took his shirt off, it was like that scene in *Crazy, Stupid, Love* where Ryan Gosling takes off his shirt and Emma Stone says, 'Fuck. Seriously? It's like you're photoshopped.' Pat had a six-pack and looked fantastic for his age. He was the first relationship I'd had outside of Chris, and it was set against the backdrop of a helpless shithole. He would ride his bike over every night, crawl into my bed and hold me until I fell asleep.

I remember laughing with Pat one morning lying in bed. I said, 'Imagine if when we were young, we cut to the future and saw this scene.' We roared with laughter at the unfathomable horror of our teenage futures, our present. Pat kept me alive for a very long time, and even when it ended, I'd replay every moment we had together in my mind. He was a great comfort when I needed it most.

*

My deepest fear was that my parents would die while I was still unwell. The thought of losing them while I was still a mess terrified me. I didn't want their last memories of me to be of tragedy and disappointment. Mum and Dad were told every time I relapsed, and I imagined it tore them apart (I may have overestimated how much they worried). After a few months of horror at the drug den, I decided to move back home with Mum and Dad. I desperately wanted to be sober and to do it under their noses. I wanted them to know where I was every night, to sleep soundly knowing I was safe. I figured, I was miserable anyway, it couldn't be any worse living with my elderly parents in my childhood home.

The three-hour drive back to Warooka was the second-worst drive of my life. The first was the 140-kilometre trip to the nearest Centrelink in Kadina to sign up for the dole a few weeks later. I was homeless, broke and signing up for welfare benefits. My sister Emily was visiting my parents at the time, and we sat in the back seat together. It was a sticky day in late summer with a hot northerly wind blowing. I was fidgeting with dread at the thought of having to line up at Centrelink. I hate queues. Thinking out loud, I said, 'God I hope there's not a queue. And if there is, I hope someone recognises me so I can skip to the front.'

Emily looked me in the eye and said, 'You're such a fuckwit. You *want* to get recognised in line at Centrelink in Kadina?' We both burst into laughter.

Not long after, we drove past an old farmhouse on the side of the road and I think I gasped at the sight of it. Mum said, 'June Barlow lives in that house. We did French lessons together. She's a big fan of both of yours. We should drop in on the way back.' I nearly jumped out of the car. Emily had to explain that's not how fan relationships work, you don't seek them out to introduce yourself. I imagined knocking on June Barlow's weathered wooden door and saying, 'Hello June, I hear *you* like me.'

Staying with my parents felt morbidly normal. I was in the throes of a total breakdown, and my mum and dad seemed oblivious to it. They went on with their everyday lives, while I fought a losing battle with the demons in my head. My mum's biggest worry at the time seemed to be her chickens. I remember fighting the urge to scream during a one-sided conversation with her.

'One of those hens' eggs hasn't been too good lately. I don't know what's wrong with her,' Mum said.

I'm having a nervous breakdown. I don't know if I'll get through the next minute, my mind raced.

'It's not too bad, just the whites are very watery,' Mum said.

I don't have a home or a cent in the bank and I've had to walk away from stand-up. There is no gig in my diary for the first time in twenty years. How will I ever go on? my mind melted.

'I guess they'll be fine scrambled, but they won't poach very well,' Mum said, in defeat.

I had no idea it could hurt this much. I need to go back to bed and curl into a ball. Maybe I can stay there forever, my mind gave up.

Lying in my childhood bed, I did curl up into a ball. We jokingly called it the Fritzl Suite because five of us had slept in there as kids, squeezed in like kidnap victims. The wallpaper was curling with age and wear, and I felt the same. Looking at the ceiling I'd spent my childhood living under, I felt as far away from home as ever. All I wanted was somewhere to call my own, a rat heaven, and I doubted I would ever have it. I was angry. I'd worked for twenty-five years and been incredibly successful. I was the woman on the stage, I was the one writing the jokes, I was the one people paid to see. How was it that I was the one who ended up penniless and destitute?

My parents took me to the local GP, who had been my doctor all my life and who I had worked under during my short nursing career. His bedside manner was blunt. He told me I needed to put on weight because I was stick and bone, and he referred me to a mental-health nurse because I was chronically depressed. He said, 'Alcoholics, yeah, generally they die alone. That's how this ends.' His frank statement sowed a seed in my mind.

I filled out a questionnaire to get on a mental-health care plan and get six free sessions with a psychologist. *'Do you have any enthusiasm for anything ever?' 'No.'* I just wanted to sleep and sleep and sleep – and never wake up.

Once again, the silence at home was deafening. There was an enormous purple elephant in the room, and no one mentioned it. Everyone carried on as normal. My visiting sister Emily was a walking reminder of everything I'd lost. She was still in the land of the living, meanwhile I was in some other sub world. I remember her standing beside my bed looking down on me. She said, 'You're going to write your way out of this.' It was a kernel of hope.

Years later, I did write about it. On stage, I said, 'When my dad walked me down the aisle at my wedding and the priest asked him, "Who gives this woman to be married to this man?" I don't remember my dad saying, "I do, but I'd really like her back when she's fifty-two and fucked up."' I performed that joke at a gig in Warooka in late 2019, and seeing my dad laugh at it filled me with unexplainable happiness. But I was nowhere near joking about my situation yet …

*

To give me a break from Mum and Dad, or to give Mum and Dad a break from me after being under their roof for almost a month, I went to stay with my sister Cate and her husband, Phil, in Port Pirie for a week. I was wearing one of Cate's daughter's dresses to go shopping. It was a summery halter-neck number. I had to put a script in at the chemist and Cate pulled up at one, telling me the girl behind the counter was a fan of mine. 'You'll make her day.'

Sure enough, when I went in, the girl was wildly excited. She asked me for a selfie, and as she lifted her phone up to a flattering angle, she stuttered awkwardly, 'Oh, um, your breast is hanging out.' The halter dress had come undone and slipped down, leaving one of my boobs completely exposed for the staff and patrons of the Port Pirie chemist to see. I was completely oblivious to the cool breeze grazing my nipple.

When I got back into the car with Cate, I told her what happened, 'Yeah, the girl was really excited, and we took a selfie. Oh, and my boob fell out of my dress.'

Cate looked at me in disbelief, 'Did that happen to you just then? And you're all right? Oh my God, if that was me I would curl into a ball of embarrassment for a week.'

To me, that moment was a tiny island off the coast of Tahiti in the global map of my humiliations. My boob hanging out in public wasn't even a blip on the radar of my shame.

*

After my infamous nip slip, I returned to the Fritzl Suite to serve out the rest of my sentence at Mum and Dad's. I was lying on my single bed when Mum came in and handed me the phone. It was Henry on the line, and he didn't have good news. Henry had been renting a room from Chris's best friend, Nick, in Alice Springs, and he was woken up early in the morning by screams from Nick's partner. Nick had had a heart attack in his sleep and his skin was cold to touch. Henry tried to give him CPR, but he was dead. He left behind his de facto wife and a young daughter, not to mention all my kids who grieved for him like a blood relative, and Chris who lost a brother. We were all devastated.

It's a strange thing to grieve for a loved one when you're in the depths of a breakdown. I knew that Nick was gone, but I couldn't feel it. My mum was beautiful when I got off the phone with Henry. I was frozen on my bed in shock. She said, 'You're allowed to cry, you know.' I'm not sure I had any tears left in me; once again, I couldn't fit any more sadness in my heart. I always told my kids, you could tell how close you were to someone if you could picture their hands. Every time I closed my eyes, I saw the lines of Nick's knuckles and the broken fourth finger that splayed slightly to the right. Oh how I wished I could have held Nick's hand in that moment. I repeated over and over, 'Don't be dead, Nick. Don't be dead, Nick.'

My mantra didn't work. You might think Nick's death would have been a wake-up call for me, a hard shake of the shoulders reminding me that life was short and precious. At the time, I do remember thinking, *For fuck's sake, Fiona, get a grip. Nick is dead. Pull yourself together.* But I couldn't.

Not long after, I returned to Adelaide to catch a flight to New Zealand for a TV appearance on a panel show called *Best Bits*. I can't remember if I'd booked the gig myself, or if it had been in the diary for some time. I do know I was in complete denial that I was up for it. Because I was still under the spell of the healer, who had been in regular contact with me since I moved back to Warooka, she decided she should come with me as a self-appointed chaperone. I didn't have any money with me, the healer kept hold of the cash for the trip. At the studio, I was under the influence of God knows what and

I completely ruined the afternoon's taping of the show. It was like I had no self-awareness. If I was pissed, I would have done what I could to hide it, but I was on something else. I thought I was fine. I wasn't. It was excruciating, apparently. My friend Lawrence Mooney, who was there, told me later, 'It was like you were on ice. That's what it looked like.' And with the healer by my side, I could well have been. Heath Franklin, the Chopper Read comedian, was there too, and he agreed with the ice assessment. Sam Mac, the *Sunrise* weatherman, was the host of the show, and now I can't watch morning TV without burning shame. I have no idea if the TV segment ever made it to air. I hope not. Or at least, I hope they edited me out.

We were in New Zealand for only two nights and I got violently ill while I was there. I was so, so sick with DTs from alcohol withdrawal. I was shaking, shivering and sweating. My heart raced. Going through customs on the way home, I thought I was going to lose bodily function in every orifice I had. I knew all I had to do was keep it straight until I got past customs. Security had spotted that I didn't look well and were asking me a thousand questions, they were very suspicious and I'm sure they were close to ripping up my ticket. I told them it was only a cold, as my hands shook and my teeth chattered with withdrawals. I was determined to get through customs.

I could see the duty-free alcohol shop, and almost taste the vodka on my tongue. I was like a heroin addict. At that point, vodka was nothing but a physical medicine. I had to get to it. I told the healer, 'I need it and I need it now.' The healer bought me a bottle and I took it to the bathroom and drank it sitting on the toilet. I vomited it straight back up and had to force myself to keep some of it down – I knew if I didn't, I would throw up on the plane, or worse, stroke out. You can die of the DTs.

When we got back to Adelaide, I returned to the drug den. My parents didn't say anything about my recrudesce. I don't think anyone knew how to handle the situation – least of all, me. Upon my return, I secretly made plans to escape. I had to act normally in front of the healer, but I was plotting to get out. I was more desperate than ever to get into a long-term rehab facility, where I could deal with all my problems and finally get better. I spoke to a high-up Catholic priest in Adelaide and asked for his help. He couldn't. I reached out to a charity I'd supported over the years that provides emergency accommodation for women experiencing homelessness in South Australia, to see if they could provide support. They couldn't. I even went to a fancy private rehab clinic in Adelaide with Sue to ask if they could waive the initial $25 000 fee and let me pay it off down the track or do publicity for them. They wouldn't.

At last, I found a room in a couple's house on a hobby farm in the Adelaide Hills. I packed my things into my carry-on suitcase – I had bugger all – and walked out the door, swearing never to return. After the Adelaide Hills, I moved in with some lesbian fans of mine, Mandy and Lee-Anne, and Mandy's son in Salisbury. I slept on a mattress on the floor of their doorless office for more than a week and then moved on to Mandy's mother Rosemary's house. I slept on a blow-up mattress in Rosemary's spare room – every morning I'd wake up with my head on the floor, the blow-up mattress having deflated in the night. I knew how it felt: flat, uncomfortable, defeated. My next stop was at a cousin's (on my dad's side). Her name is Angela and her kindnesses to me over the years are numerous. Last on my list of prerecovery postcodes was a room in a beautiful share house, which Sue had organised for me, living with a group of medical students back in Glenelg. It was crazy cheap because it was a tiny room. It wasn't a 'rat heaven', but it was something. The owner of the house knew who I was and asked Sue, 'Why would Fiona O'Loughlin want to rent a room for seventy-five dollars a week?'

Sue made an excuse, 'Oh, she's writing a novel and only needs one bedroom for the time she's in Adelaide.' Bit by bit, the medical students cottoned on. They realised they were living with a live one.

The first night I was there I had a cigarette in the backyard with the bloke who was renting the granny flat out the back of the house. His name was Ben and he was a chef. He knew exactly what he was looking at because his mother had been an active alcoholic. He said, 'I don't know you, but I've never seen a sadder woman in my life.' I felt the same way every time I looked in the mirror. Ben kept an eye on me and tried to make me promise not to drink each day. I couldn't keep any promises. I was hocking my belongings at Cash Converters to scrounge enough money to buy vodka and escape. My reality was intolerable to live in. I was barely existing.

With help from Ben and Sue, I finally managed to get into a psych ward in the autumn of 2016. Ben called my sister Cate and she came straightaway. It's a three-hour drive from Port Pirie to Glenelg, but she was there first thing in the morning. Cate walked in wearing a houndstooth jacket, all casual, middle-class, middle-aged lady wear. The contrast between her outfit and mine struck me between the eyes. I looked down at what I was wearing: a blue-and-white floral dress teamed with an orange-and-green waistcoat. I looked at her, and back at me, and said, 'Oh Cate, would you have a look at me.'

She put her hand out like a stop sign and said, 'Oh, it's perfect.' I looked as crazy as I felt. I was admitted to Glenside Psychiatric Hospital that night.

It might sound strange, but my stay at Glenside was lovely. It was the safest I had felt in a long time. I had my own room, with a thin, springless, plastic-covered mattress, and three basic meals a day. It was previously known as the Parkside Lunatic Asylum, and I knew I was where I belonged.

CHAPTER 9

VOLUNTARILY MAD

Rehab is exactly like it is in the movies. For the first time in my life, my reality lived up to my TV expectations. After waiting at the Glenside Psychiatric Hospital for five weeks in 2016, I was given a place at a therapeutic community adult program in Canberra. My heart was full of hope. I knew I needed to be in a public centre with a 12-step program, and this rehab clinic ticked those boxes. I'd been in so many private clinics and they *clearly* hadn't worked for me. At those centres, I was never forced to look at myself and tell the ugly truth; and that's the real work of recovery. On stage,

I joke about the time I've spent in psych wards, 'I quite like being institutionalised and I don't mind custard, so I never put up a fight.'

The place I'd signed up for was one of the toughest rehab centres in the country. There would be no joking about custard. I was one of only a handful of people there voluntarily. Everyone else was either admitted under a court order to get their kids back from the welfare department, or as a last resort instead of jail. In my five months there, I saw three people come in and choose jail over this clinic.

The program was based on the 12 steps of Alcoholics Anonymous and to my mind had nailed a lot of what an alcoholic needs to address. Not that I could fully appreciate it at the time.

Step 1: We admitted we were powerless over alcohol – that our lives had become unmanageable.
Step 2: We came to believe and accept that we needed strengths beyond our awareness and resources to restore us to sanity.
Step 3: We made a decision to entrust our will and our lives to the care of the collective wisdom and resources of those who have searched before us.

Step 4: We made a searching and fearless moral inventory of ourselves.

Step 5: We admitted to ourselves, without reservation, and to another human being the exact nature of our wrongs.

Step 6: We were ready to accept help in letting go of all our defects of character.

Step 7: With humility and openness, we sought to eliminate our shortcomings.

Step 8: We made a list of all persons we had harmed and became willing to make amends to them all.

Step 9: We made direct amends to such people wherever possible, except when to do so would injure them or others.

Step 10: We continued to take personal inventory and when we were wrong, promptly admitted it.

Step 11: We sought through meditation to improve our spiritual awareness and our understanding of the AA way of life and to discover the power to carry out that way of life.

Step 12: Having had a spiritual awakening as a result of these steps, we tried to carry this message to alcoholics and to practise these principles in all our affairs.

I caught a bus from Adelaide to Canberra. Once again, I couldn't afford a flight. My sisters Genevieve and Sarah and my son Bert, then twenty-two, waved me off. Bert's face was the last thing I saw as we drove away. He looked relieved. Staring out the window on the familiar drive along the South Australian coast, I wondered what that young woman on the McCafferty's bus heading to Melbourne to watch stand-up would think of me now. If only she knew. If only I could have warned her. If only.

I stashed alcohol in my bag to drink on the bus. I'd secretly been stocking up while I was at Glenside, going to the IGA across the road and buying tiny bottles of Jack Daniel's Black Label and Bombay Sapphire Gin. Because I was at Glenside by choice (or as I like to call it, 'voluntarily mad'), I was free to come and go from the centre. I giggled to myself as I hid my top-shelf stash in my bag. It was a last hurrah and I was going out in Black Label style – I didn't even consider buying vodka; that was an everyday drink, not a special-occasion liquor.

On stage, I used to joke about the kind of people who took buses instead of flights: 'If you find yourself catching a coach over the age of thirty-five, you pretty much know you're a disappointment to yourself and your family. People on buses aren't happy people and they're about forty per cent uglier than people on planes. And if you think the people on buses are ugly, you should see the people at the other end meeting the people on buses. A bus is just a moving capsule of losers.

All the winners are flying right over the top of us.' Alanis Morissette would have loved the irony.

When I arrived at the rehab clinic nineteen hours later, in the dead of night, I was shaky with a hangover from my last hurrah. Pulling up at the facility was like arriving at a low-security prison. But instead of prison guards, they have loving staff who are mostly former addicts themselves living in recovery. The staff searched my bags on arrival – they didn't find anything because I'd downed it all two states earlier – and showed me to my room. I was allowed one day to settle in. The morning after that, I was thrown into rehab life. I had no idea what I'd got myself into. I was shaky again, this time with fear.

In the beginning of my time there, I was a quiet shell of a human as I went through withdrawals. For the first six weeks, you don't go to group therapy, touch on feelings or talk about your childhood. The case workers introduce you to the program with basic training to teach you about how substances affect your body and brain. Those first six weeks were like a holding pen where the staff recalibrate you physically before they hit you with the hard stuff. They ease you into it, before they ask you if you felt loved as a child.

The sleeping quarters were called mods. I was in a mod with five other women, separated into three bedrooms. The sheets were horrendously cheap flannels in lovely hues of purple, pink and lime green. I shared a room with a transgender man named Jacob and a woman called Lynda. She was like a character I couldn't make up. She looked like Lizzie Birdsworth from *Prisoner*, with grey features, a toothless smile and deep wrinkles. Her arms were as thick as her legs. When I found out she was younger than me, I was horrified. Lynda was every bit as cunning as Lizzie Birdsworth too. Her mind only bothered itself with the misgivings of others and trivial dramas she created. If rehab were a town, she would be the town gossip. She had no teeth and she would scrounge around her bed in the middle of the night for toffees that she would suck on until she fell asleep. The first night I slept in the same room as her, I thought it was a rat. I'll never be able to unhear the sound of a toothless alcoholic sucking and swallowing toffee juice, her tongue wriggling around her mouth like an eel. I remember thinking, *If only my sisters were here with me and we could laugh at the absurdity of this situation.* If only. My coping mechanism, as always, was to find the humour in the darkness. I told myself, 'This is brief. It's a moment in time. And it's hilarious.'

The facility was like a one-star family motel on the side of a regional highway with sweeping views of a carpark. It smelled like a hospital, all antiseptic and bleach, but it didn't feel like an institution. It didn't feel like home, either. I imagined it was once a rambling homestead, but now it felt like the kind of place accountants in cheap suits would go for a working conference weekend of team-building exercises and scavenger hunts. The well-worn carpet was a calming shade of blue and the walls were a yellowy cream. All the furniture was donated and second-hand, so nothing matched; there was no uniform aesthetic. The cupboard next to my single bed was a ramshackle piece of bric-à-brac. The furnishings were much like the residents: misfits and rejects with chipped edges and stiff joints.

The routine was the same every day. Up at 7 am to clean the mod, mop the floors, do the laundry and scrub the toilet. The toilets were cleaned every single day. They sparkled. After half an hour of duties, we had breakfast in the communal eating area. Breakfast was my favourite part of the day. Eating when you're hungry after so long without an appetite feels fantastic. After breakfast, we would get on with the rest of our duties and our recovery. We had daily AA meetings and group therapy, plus one-on-one counselling sessions. We spent a minimum of four hours on recovery each day, with the main goal of drumming it into us that we can never, ever, *ever* drink. For dinner, the Irish chef would cook all the things that make you feel happy: potatoes, roasts and schnitzels, all slathered in gravy. I knew I would get as fat as a pig if I wasn't careful, so I halved everything I ate. Bedtime was 9 pm and I would sleep like a log, physically exhausted from the hours of peeling potatoes and mentally exhausted from the hours of peeling back layers of my psyche.

In rehab, our time was not our own. We were all responsible for the running of the joint and were assigned duties that rotated every six weeks between cleaning, cooking and gardening, which was my dreaded fear. I'm the opposite of a gardener. As you know, I'm incredibly lazy and only do things so I can eventually go back to doing nothing. Physical labour leaves me cold. Plus, I hate being outside.

We had one hour to ourselves after dinner and before lights out. I never knew what to do with my precious sixty minutes, I was overwhelmed with options. Do I read? Do I pluck my eyebrows? Do I sit in my thoughts and relish in the hour of freedom? I desperately missed lounging on a couch – my favourite pastime. But I understood that the heavily structured routine was about teaching us complete focus. We had to learn that recovery was life or death. There was no time for bullshit.

The rules were as rigid as the routine. We weren't allowed to watch TV; in fact, there weren't any TVs to watch. We weren't allowed to have phones or computers. We could write letters to our loved ones, and we had three nights a week when we could make a ten-minute phone call – but only to one of the three people on our list. If we wanted to call someone else, we had to put in a written request and give two weeks' notice. It was all about delaying instant gratification. Because I understood the logic behind the rules, I had no reason to arc up about anything.

As you would expect, violence of any kind was forbidden. So, too, were romantic relationships with other inmates – sorry, clients. We weren't allowed to be alone in a room with just one other client, we always had to be in groups. The ramifications for breaking the rules ranged from having to clean up the kitchen alone to being sent to a demountable outside to spend twenty-four hours in isolation. I never dared step out of line.

We also had the responsibility of holding each other accountable. If you saw anyone break the rules, you had to 'concern' them, which meant they had to write in a book that they were concerned about their transgression, which could have been something as simple as leaving a mug in their mod rather than taking it back to the kitchen to wash it up, or talking about another client behind their back. Of course, it felt like dobbing, but it also instilled a sense of responsibility and camaraderie. We were in this together.

On Saturdays, we were driven by bus to Coles for our weekly shopping outing. I had to restrain myself from licking the windows as a joke. We had between $10 and $50 on a rehab card – we were literally card-carrying lunatics – and were only ever allowed to get what was on our shopping list, which had to be written and submitted ahead of time. On my first shopping trip, I felt like I was in chains. Another consequence of the blind, stubborn ignorance in me that refused to put down the bloody bottle. I couldn't even buy a bottle of conditioner on a whim or a spontaneous packet of chips. What had my life come to?

At the time, Nestlé – God bless them – had brought out a salted-caramel KitKat. It was my weekly treat, and the thought of tearing open the red wrapper was too exciting for words. If I didn't get a salted-caramel KitKat or a mini twin-pack of salted caramel Tim Tams, I would get a finger bun with soft, creamy icing – and no sultanas. There's a time and place for sultanas, and it's not in finger buns. The best bit? A finger bun was only $1, so I could buy two if I didn't get the new copy of *New Idea*.

Our group therapy sessions were every bit as dramatic as I imagined after watching *One Flew Over the Cuckoo's Nest*. We started by checking in with each other – 'Hi, my name is Fiona and I'm an alcoholic. Today I'm feeling sad because

I miss my kids.' Then we would get to the root of the emotions we were feeling. It was all about going through the wreckage of your past and trying to make sense of it where possible. We learned that not everything you face can be sorted, but nothing can be sorted if it's not faced. Group therapy was not a place to sit and roll around in your resentments. It was not a place to throw confetti in the air at your personal pity party. It was not a place for competition. No one's story was worse. We were all as tragic as each other. AA applause all round.

The people I met in rehab were some of the most incredible people I've ever known. As their stories revealed themselves in group therapy, I was enthralled. It was interesting to me that everyone's story started the same: we all had a hole in our soul and found temporary relief with alcohol, drugs, self-harm or disordered eating. Sitting in the circle, I heard stories that broke my heart.

There was a couple who had been sentenced to eighteen months in rehab instead of serving a prison sentence for child neglect. They were so middle-class, so normal and so incredibly good-looking. They would have been in their forties and had their own business, kids and a nice house in a good suburb. A decade earlier, they had gone to a party and tried ice for the first time. They were so struck by the power of it and, unknown to the other, they both started to use it regularly. They were addicted at the very first taste. When they realised that the other one was using as well, they became each other's co-dependants and enablers. It was them against the world, fighting their way through a drug haze to get whatever gear they could. It was the same old story: it was fantastic until it was awful. Their lives spiralled out of control. They lost their children. They lost their business. They were sent to rehab. The wife's parents had to look after the couple's kids. I would look at the wife and think, *Where is your mind?* The same place as mine, I guess.

The wife's name was 'Sarah'. I almost couldn't breathe trying to wrap my head around her inner guilt. She and her husband were taking their medicine graciously, but they literally had years of hardship ahead of them before they would regain access to their children. I came up with a plan and took it to my case manager. 'I'll be free in six months or so. I could rent a place here in Canberra and have their kids live with me so they'll be able to see them every day when they get out of here,' I pleaded my case. I waited for my case manager's reaction. I was bursting at the seams to tell Sarah the good news. My case manager must have had a rough day – and I might have been the final straw – but she told me bluntly and severely that my co-dependency was going to kill me quicker than my alcoholism, and sent me packing with two books on the subject to be read within the week. I'll never forget Sarah. Her youngest child was a toddler.

Then there was 'Richard', who had been homeless since he was sixteen. He was thirty-five when I met him. I'll never forget the day he arrived at the clinic. He was this very tall, very thin man, and as I watched him being admitted, he vomited the brightest green bile I've ever seen. He was detoxing, hard. Richard was the son of a single mother. They didn't have much when he was little, but they got by. When his mum remarried, Richard got on with his stepfather – until they had their own natural children. The stepfather started abusing Richard horrifically. He left home, lived on the streets and became addicted to heroin. He was such a kind and loving man. When I had another tooth pulled out (which was now a huge trigger for me), Richard held my hand all the way back to rehab from the dental surgery in the bus. I'll never forget the comfort I felt having him beside me.

I caught up with Richard twice after I left rehab. Both times were after gigs in Canberra where Richard proudly paid to see me perform. I vividly remember running into his arms in the carpark of the Canberra Theatre Centre, where we inhaled each other happily. I had wanted to tell him I was still struggling, but I was too eager to hear about how well he was doing. This incredibly tall and empathetic man was living in the light for the first time in his adult life. Of everyone in rehab, I didn't see anyone work the program as hard as Richard did. Some time ago I was chatting to one of my rehab friends who still lives in Canberra and I asked about Richard. 'I saw him the other day begging out the front of Coles,' they told me.

During the program, I also became friends with my roommate, the transgender man, who was born as a girl called Jess and went by the name 'Jacob'. As a child, Jacob's heroin-addict mum kept him and his brother as slaves and sold them for sex for a fix. They never had a Christmas. They only had each other. When they finally escaped their mother as young adults and moved into a place together, Jacob woke up one morning and found his brother hanging in the backyard. Understandably, he broke down under the weight of his loss and trauma, and he turned to alcohol to cope with the pain. He was in rehab to get dry and to make plans to physically transition to a man. When I looked at Jacob, I only ever saw a boy. His eyes were the eyes of a boy. He was a boy.

I learned as much from the people at rehab as I did from the program itself, which I think is the intention. I feel honoured to know the people I met and to be a part of their community. Rehab is such a leveller; I now know that no one is better than anyone else, we all go through shit, we all have demons, and we all need kindness.

*

Three months into my stay, I was sitting outside the office waiting to fill out some paperwork when my body was overtaken by an extreme physical urge to drink. The urge was too big for my body, so I jumped around and banged on the reception door. I cried and begged and demanded a drink. I was so embarrassed by my request, but the urge was stronger than my shame. It was the first time my disease had attacked me while my mind was at peace. This time, it wasn't the voice in my head telling me I needed a bottle of vodka, it was a physical force. I nearly jumped out the window to try to satisfy the itch.

My treatment had been going so well, I was more shocked than anyone at my sudden need. The staff just looked at me, knowingly, and said, 'Oh yeah, this is something that happens. You've just got to ride it out.' Fighting physical and mental urges was all part of the process. Like all diseases, my alcoholism had a job to do, and that job was to kill me. My job was to fight back, to stay strong, to live.

As much as I was ashamed about the desperate compulsion, it was a moment of realisation. It was the first time I'd been in a position where I couldn't satisfy my urge. I knew if I had been on the outside, I would have relapsed. I went to bed that night feeling overwhelmingly grateful to be there, in my small room, with my itchy blanket, listening to Lynda's heavy breathing. Rehab saved me from myself.

*

Getting a letter in rehab was like finding gold. I received beautiful letters from my kids and friends, and I would read them over and over again, relishing every delicious word from the outside world. Genevieve wrote me a detailed recollection of Henry's thirtieth birthday party in Alice Springs, which I couldn't attend for obvious reasons, but reading her letter made me feel a part of the day. During my third month in Canberra, a letter arrived from Chris and my heart skipped at the sight of his familiar handwriting. I imagined him sitting down at our hardwood dining table in Alice Springs to write it, his serious eyebrows furrowed in concentration, trying to find the right words. I don't know what I was expecting, but when I read the letter at the start of our daily group therapy session, I was overcome with disappointment. It was a single-page perfunctory note telling me something obligatory. I read it again searching for something personal, something heartfelt, anything. He started the letter with, *'I've got to make this quick.'* Click went the trigger. The first and longest battle we fought had been the battle for his time. Chris swore he didn't have it to give and I swore that it wasn't enough. It felt like I still wasn't worth more than five minutes of his attention. I started crying. My case manager saw how broken I was and took me outside, away from the group. When I showed her the letter, she immediately understood and let me go back to my mod (which was rare) so I could be by myself and cry it out.

I rolled around on my bedroom floor and wailed in grief. Sounds came out of me that I'd never heard before. That single line, *'I've got to make this quick,'* made me realise how alone I was in the world. I didn't have anyone. There was no partner waiting for me on the outside.

The last time I cried like that was at the Albert Road Clinic in 2015 after my carbon-monoxide poisoning. It was as though

I allowed myself to break down in tears of self-pity once a year. Just before I left Alice Springs, I remember collapsing into a heap (literally) of dirty laundry on the bathroom floor. I had to be in a car on the way to the airport in twenty minutes to catch a flight for work, and all of my clothes were wet in the washing machine. The pressure of having five kids, a career, a life-threatening disease and no clean undies pushed me over the edge. I was sobbing on the floor saying, 'You poor thing, you poor thing.'

After half an hour of guttural crying in my mod, another case manager came into my room and told me I had ten more minutes and then I had to go back to group therapy. I thought, *Jesus, that's a bit rough. I've just had a meltdown. Surely I can have the rest of the afternoon off?* But alas, recovery waits for no one. I wiped my tears away and splashed my red face with water before I re-joined the session.

That night, I had a weird psychic moment, which happens to me every now and then. I was lying in bed, dozing off to sleep to the sound of Lynda sucking on her toffees and I heard a voice in my mind calling out to me. It was my granddaughter from the future; she was saying, 'Noni, I need you.'

Two years later, Tess gave birth to my granddaughter Úna Mary Dunne, and she calls me Noni.

*

Halfway through my rehab stint, I had a visit from Tess, Jasmin and Mary-Anne. One Sunday a month, clients were allowed visitors, but because I wasn't from Canberra, I never had anyone drop by – until that day. I woke up like a little kid on Christmas morning, bursting with excitement and anticipation. Every five minutes, I peeped through the curtains hoping to see them outside.

Of course, it was amazing to see them all. We hugged and we cried, then we hugged and cried some more. They told me how well I looked, which was deeply reassuring – and made their imminent goodbye bearable.

The hardest part of rehab for me was confronting the hurt I'd caused my children. I made a huge mess during their formative years and took away their sense of ease. That's something I can never give them back. I dread to think about the number of nights they spent wide awake not knowing where their mother was; if she was safe or passed out alone in a foreign city. Of course I've apologised to them, but making amends is a process. Once I asked Bert to tell me what it was like for him, and he sent me this beautiful piece he'd written for a university assignment …

THE EARLY YEARS IN MELBOURNE

Mary was living in Prahran in 2013 with our mother as
she began Year 10. All her siblings had boarded in South
Australia for their remaining three years at school. But Mary
was given a different choice, she could board like the rest in
Adelaide, or she could follow Mum and move to Melbourne
from Alice Springs and 'start again'. She loved to sing and
dance and make films on the weekends and do watercolours
in her room, and we were all joyed that she'd made the right
decision. Mum would be happier there and Mary would be
happy being with a happy mother.

They lived in an art deco apartment in Prahran. The
exterior walls were rendered white and stood beside tall
Arborvitae trees. They had wooden floorboards, leadlight
windows, a bright sunroom and still-working fireplaces. It was
a fault of Mum's that she often felt she had to buy our love.
Still, she thought she was sure to win on the day that Mary
moved in. Unfortunately, Mary couldn't quite shake out her
inner cashed-up bogan on the three-hour flight to Melbourne.
Anything less than completely modern was 'disgusting'. She
had a knack for spitting in the face of something. Perhaps
it was because Mum spoiled her, but we found it deliciously
funny. 'What the fuck? I can see the pipes in the bathroom!'

During the 2009 Melbourne Comedy Festival, Mary and I came down from Alice Springs to stay for a week while Mum was doing her show in the Town Hall. We got put up in a lower than average hotel and twelve-year-old Mary didn't fail to entertain. She screamed her way from room to room while Mum and I rolled with laughter in the lounge. 'They don't have a Bible in the top drawer!'

'Why do you need a Bible, Mary?'

'I don't! But they just should have one!'

The year started fine, Mary enjoyed her school and Mum seemed to be going quite well – 'It's gonna be so much better not having to travel everywhere and stay in shitty hotels every other night! That's where the temptation comes. When I'm alone in a hotel and there's a mini-bar and nothing else. Now I can just do my shows, come home and have a cup of tea!'

It didn't matter much to us that Mum and Dad had separated. When I spoke to Mary about it we agreed that it actually made a lot of sense after a little while. I think mostly because there was something much larger lingering behind their separation that we were more concerned about. But, for the moment, we were happy that both Mum and Dad still asked of the other, happy that we'd overhear friendly phone calls every now and then and happy that we didn't have to avoid talking about one or the other to either. All we were terrified of was how long it would be until that horrible woman would come knocking at our front door again.

And she always comes without warning, and always with a storm behind her back. You could sometimes make out her slow, slouching footsteps thump up the stairs, or at least her stench. Other times you jumped with terror at the sudden strong, invasive knock on the front door. And your heart sank, your eyes filled with tears and you wanted to sink into the floor and scream until you didn't feel so alone.

'Six months today! Woo-hoo!' Mum boasts to Mary, though I knew it was less and it hurt that she knew that I knew, and could still happily lie to my younger sister in front of me. While I was living in Adelaide, only two months earlier, I'd received a phone call from my friend and housemate, Clancy, saying that I needed to come home because Mum didn't look too good – knock, knock – I left a family dinner on Dad's side and came home to find her poorly dressed and passed out on the couch outside. Clancy had gone to sleep. So I laid her down in my bed and cried beside her until I dozed off as well.

'Well done!'

'Thankin' yoo, Mary-Agnes!'

There were five in the Prahran house: Mary, Mum, our sister Tess, her new Irish boyfriend Ciarán and myself. Soon Tess and Ciarán would move to London and I back home to Alice Springs and we'd leave poor Mary on her own. I couldn't imagine doing that now. One afternoon I got a phone call from Mum's manager to say that she was in Port Fairy and had fallen off the wagon. Her manager was forty-two years old and had known her for a long time, but still handballed it off to me. Tess was in London at this point. My other sister Biddy called and told me how sorry she was that I had to go, but that just made me more upset. It was easier to pretend it was a dream. I got to Port Fairy and a woman named Tina picked me up and took me to her house where Mum was. She was quite old, had a tremendously husky voice and was far too chirpy. I say that because of the situation we were in; she didn't seem like a naturally chirpy person but she was clearly somewhat chuffed at the fact that she found herself in this position.

'I'm a big fan of your mum's!' she said proudly

'Ahh ...' I faltered, after staring blindly through the car window. 'Thank you.'

'She's sooo funny! Ha! What's it like? Having a comedian as a mother?' I think she'd forgotten that my mother was currently blind drunk in her house and I was there to pick her up. 'Is she funny at home as well?'

'Yeah, she is.'

I double took as I noticed her stare on me, and not the road, smiling, but with the corners of her mouth turned down 'She's vvvery funny!'

Her house was dark, had plenty of unopened bottles of alcohol in the kitchen and smelled like toilet freshener. It was horrible. I still think of that night whenever I come across the smell. An odd host is the beer garden at The Old Bar, so I prefer The Evelyn when I find myself in Fitzroy.

Mum and I arrived home to Prahran, I was wrecked and resolved to take the job with my uncle in Alice Springs and spend the remainder of my gap year up there. Biddy was in an apartment not far from Prahran, so we knew it would be okay. It was terrible saying goodbye to Mary, we both cried a lot but she understood that I couldn't hang around looking after Mum.

The rest of the year went on. Mary found a dear group of friends who she spoke about often and she told me how happy she was that she'd found a school that was so heavily focused on the arts. But, as we knew very well, that woman had an unrelenting urge to strike that door twice more. Nothing would do but to simply knock. Twice. And the longing was gone. It had to be done. During one of Mary's classes, she received a suicide message from Mum that was sent to all of us. Her friends kept talking beside her, the teacher still paced the front of the room but everything slowed and became a blur, like a moving impressionist painting, though dark. And it was as if they were put there by her own mind in order to make everything seem like it was going on as normal. As though she could wipe them all away as she pleased. But all she could do at that moment was panic in silence, surrounded by all that noise and all that colour. I hate to think of the image of her putting her phone away after reading the text, to see her face and the terror that was ripping through her mind at that moment, because most kids would run straight to the door after reading a text like that. But we didn't. We'd seen these messages before and so instead we began to feel numb. Our brain didn't want to deal with the trauma again so it shut off. For Mary, it took time before she felt as deadened as the rest of us. She used to jump into the joys of seeing Mum sober and happy, and when terrible times came she cried and screamed for her innocence. Now, she had those terrible moments of watching that darkness fill her mind before she could make a decision. She told her teacher that she had to leave. Nobody knew exactly where Mum was but she knew she wasn't far from Prahran. After thirty minutes of searching, Mary marched down Commercial Road and walked into a motel. The receptionist confirmed that there was a person matching Mum's description who checked in earlier. She was sixteen and unaccompanied and completely undeterred by the thought of what she might find at the top of that building. She asked the receptionist to let her into Mum's room. He replied saying he's 'not really meant to do that' and immediately took her upstairs after a second glance at the broken sixteen-year-old.

An ambulance was called and Mum woke the next day in the hospital. It was hard to feel sorry for her but we did. They sent her back to the Albert Road Clinic, a common visiting point for us during that time, a place that we looked upon with a lot of hope in the early years, but it soon turned grey and soulless.

She will always live in Mum, at the bottom of the stairs. And she will forever long to knock. Twice.

All of my kids have stories like Bert's. The monster inside me has knocked, twice, on all of their doors. If I thought it would banish that horrible woman at the bottom of the stairs forever, I would chop off my hands so I could never knock again.

*

I didn't expect to fall in love in rehab. Then again, I didn't expect to end up in rehab at all after living in a drug den and losing everything at age fifty-two. But there I was ... I met 'Dave' in the kitchen. We were a real snap. He was everything I'd ever wanted in a man. He was astonishingly funny, well educated in politics and history, and he was a very straight shooter. Dave was the king of rehab in many ways; he had been at the clinic eight years earlier for a long-term heroin addiction and had relapsed on ice. He was powerful in the way he described how shitful that drug is. His interactions with everyone were genuine, warm and profound. Outside rehab, Dave was a stonemason, which I found terribly romantic. I'd stare at his rough, manly hands. And his tattoos. And his handsome stubbled face.

Perving aside, it was Dave's mind that I fell in love with. I started having an illicit romance with him in my head. The minute I realised my feelings were reciprocated, we had so much fun. We'd sneak moments hidden around corners and communicate in code in front of the other clients. We would ache with laughter when we were together. Dave was a match for all the comedians I knew. Sometimes you find one out in the wild, an uncut gem who has mastered the art of storytelling and comedic timing on the streets instead of on the stage. Because we weren't allowed to read anything that wasn't recovery based, I would read out pamphlets on addiction in ridiculous accents when we were on kitchen duty together. I'd be Rick from *The Young Ones*, before breaking into hysterical giggles like a blushing schoolgirl with a crush.

For a brief moment in time, my slate with the world was clean. At rehab, I wasn't an arsehole, I hadn't hurt anyone, people liked me – a lot. I was eating well, and my body and mind had never been better. On the outside, I was such a time waster with odd compulsions – I'd play a game on my phone for eight hours to waste the day away – but at rehab I was focused and had purpose. I loved working in the kitchen, mostly because of Dave, but still.

My case worker and I spoke a lot about my co-dependency and how it enabled my alcoholism. She told me I relied excessively on other people for approval and a sense of identity. I learned I needed to overcome my co-dependence in order to overcome my alcoholism. They were the same, single voice in my head, telling me that I wasn't good enough, not funny enough, not enough full-stop.

After five months in rehab, my feelings for Dave became all-consuming. I fell hard. I physically couldn't bear to be in the same room as him and not be able to reach out and stroke his face or kiss his cheek or curl up in his lap. It was torture. I knew I had to leave. When I was admitted, I only planned on spending six months in rehab, so it wasn't as though I was tapping out ridiculously early. I was happy with the progress I had made, and genuinely thought Dave and I could make a go of it on the outside. I told my case manager about Dave – I had a feeling she already knew. I doubt our stolen moments and lovelorn glances were as secret as we thought. My case manager made a comment about Dave not being good enough for me. 'Don't sell yourself short, Fiona,' she said. She was wrong.

The last thing my case manager said to me was, 'Please work on your co-dependency. If you don't sort that, your alcoholism will never be sorted.' She was right.

Dave and I didn't get to speak properly before I left, because there were eyes everywhere, but I knew we would have plenty of time to talk on the outside when he finished his treatment plan.

Free from rehab, I caught a flight from Canberra to Melbourne and stayed with Tess. She'd found me a beautiful apartment on the seventh floor of a picturesque building on Collins Street in the CBD. It was only a small one bedder, but it had a luxurious bay window overlooking the city, French windows, high ceilings and hard floors. I couldn't believe my luck. I had fantasies about lounging around with Dave admiring the view together when he got out of rehab.

I was back on stage within weeks of returning to Melbourne. I had to be – after getting set up in my new apartment, I had exactly $1.40 to my name. I'd been out of the game for eighteen months, so I accepted whatever gig was going, getting most of my work through the generous grapevine of other comics. I cancelled my first scheduled gig at the last minute because I just wasn't ready. So, my first gig back ended up being a spot at a drag queen bingo night. It paid $200. I was very nervous – as I had every right to be – but I've never doubted my ability to do my job. The drag queen bingo felt like a soft place to land. For some reason, I resonate with the gay community and I feel very safe in their company. My friend and fellow comedian Joel Creasey was in the audience and he was excited, which made me excited. For good luck I wore the jacket I had lived in when I was doing it tough in Adelaide. It was a reminder that if I could survive living in a drug den, I could survive twenty minutes on stage. And I did, and I did. When I got the first laughs, I remember the rush of warmth I felt. There's nothing like it.

The gigs started trickling in and I was making enough money to get by, counting down the moments until I could see Dave and we could reignite our romance in the real world.

Dave left rehab a couple of months after me. I was desperate to see him, but when he got out of the rehab bubble, things weren't the same. I had been so wrapped up in my own thoughts and dreams, I forgot that Dave had a life of his own in Canberra. I reached out to him, only to hear silence. I tried to see him, only to be stopped. I tried to make sense of what was happening, only to upset myself. I think Dave thought having an actual relationship with me in the outside world was beyond the realm of possibility. He was an addict stonemason in Canberra, and I was an alcoholic comedian in Melbourne. I found out through a mutual friend we both met at rehab that Dave was still going strong and sober after rehab. Though, he had started living like a recluse, shut off from the world and me. I wish him well, but I know I will miss him forever.

I don't have a long and varied history of relationships. I guess Chris, Pat and Dave are a pretty fine collection all things considered. Once again, I didn't get the romcom I'd dreamed of watching TV. My 'happy ending' was just an ordinary fade-to-black. Roll the credits. Fin. I felt weirdly comforted in my loss. I listened to Sarah McLachlan's song 'Angel' on repeat and let myself feel glorious sadness. Nobody knew about my heartache, and it didn't consume me, but it was a loss that I recognised and enjoyed a *Bridget Jones* movie over. For the first time in the longest time, I felt a simple sadness that had no place for shame nor guilt.

When things ended with Dave (not that they ever really began), I became promiscuous. After being with the same man for all of my adult life, I had a handful of one-night stands. I wasn't looking for a relationship and I certainly wasn't looking for sex, I just cared less about myself. I was trying to fill an emotional hole by filling a physical hole. Spoiler alert: it didn't work. Now the men are just blurred regrets in the back of my mind. I can't remember any of their names or faces, and I certainly couldn't pick them in a line-up. It wasn't fun, it was desperate. Worse, it was self-flagellation.

I don't regret leaving rehab when I did even though things didn't work out with Dave. Something in my gut told me it was the right time to go, and it was. Rehab was everything I had prayed it would be. There is a distinct line between my life before rehab and after. Something changed in me there. I knew I still had a long way to go, but I was heading in the right direction. And I knew I wasn't going to go backwards. I was grateful to have a roof over my head, a job to keep me going and visits from my kids.

I remember lying in bed reading *New Idea* listening to Henry, then thirty, and Mary-Agnes, eighteen, talking in the lounge room. They are my bookends – and Henry's nurturing of his younger sister is beautiful.

The closeness of my kids made me smile to myself, thinking at least I got one thing in my life right – even if it was by total accident and probably had a lot more to do with my kids than me. Turning the page of the magazine to admire Kim Kardashian's impressive arse, everything felt right in the world. If only for a moment.

CHAPTER 10

IT'S A JUNGLE OUT THERE

U P UNTIL 2018, I HAD NEVER LOST A DEBATE. My very first debate was in Alice Springs against a professor in Indigenous studies. It wasn't a comedic debate, but a serious one. The topic was 'From the Desert Prophets Come', and I was affirmative. I used all the imagery and humour I'd collected over my years living in the desert and crowbarred jokes and colour into my speech. The audience lapped it up. When I beat the academic professor, I became quite competitive about it. I started doing as many comedic debates as I could and my winning streak continued. Usually the ideas came to me a day before the debate. I'd form my arguments into something that resembled a speech and add in as many jokes as possible in my allotted time.

At the 2014 Melbourne International Comedy Festival, Amanda Keller introduced me by saying, 'When it comes to fighting evil spirits, there's no one more qualified than Fiona O'Loughlin.' The topic was 'Is it Okay to Fake it?', and I was on the affirmative team with Tom Gleeson and Joel Creasey, against Cal Wilson, Doc Brown and Jason Byrne. I opened my second-speaker speech with, 'I'm not going to lower the tone of this debate with a *When Harry Met Sally* moment. I actually have never faked an orgasm because I've never had one. Although, I have had thrush and the house to myself, so I think I get the drift.

'Of course we all fake it,' I continued, 'we're all comedians. And before I was a comedian, my stage was the dinner party. And I loved holding court at dinner parties. Unfortunately, I was married to someone who was normal. He used to interrupt me in the middle of a great story to pull me up with the truth, which I found annoying. Little things, like, "Fiona, you've never actually been to Sweden," and, "Van Morrison isn't really your first cousin."

'We've all had to fake it as comedians. I was the only female comedian ever to perform in Port Moresby – and possibly the last. I got there, I did my performance. The audience was completely made up of businessmen and politicians. Unfortunately, what they had been expecting at the Holiday Inn in Port Moresby was a stripper. So, God knows what was going through their brains as I was regaling them with stories about my last caesarean section. They must have been thinking, *Well, this is all very interesting. When's she going to get her kit off?* And I didn't. Afterwards the CEO of the mining company came up to me and said, "That was lovely, but we were actually expecting something a little more raunchy." He was winking at me, which was strange. I said, "I don't really do anything raunchy." Maybe he thought I was a reluctant stripper. He got a bit desperate. And he said, "Is there anything you can do that's a bit raunchy?" And talk about faking it, there was a guitarist there, so I said, "Maybe I could sing a song." His eyes lit up. He said, "Hell, if you can sing a song and sing it raunchy, I'll get my accountant to go downstairs and get you $1000." So, before I knew it, I was standing on top of a table singing "House of the Rising Sun" with a bit of hip movement. I didn't even know the words to "House of the Rising Sun", so I made them up. You can't fake it more than that, ladies and gentlemen,' I closed my speech, and promptly got up on my team's table in my nude heels and lacy red dress, and sang my raunchy version of 'House of the Rising Sun', complete with hip movements and a bass guitarist. The crowd cheered and hooted. We won.

A few months after I got out of rehab, I was booked for a debate with my friend Lawrence Mooney in Ballarat. It was the first real test of my sobriety. As I made my way down Collins Street to the train station bound for the gig, I started to panic. Normally, the ideas would have come to me by then and I would have written a speech in my head. The debate was three hours away and my mind was empty. It was a very easy topic, and I was drawing a complete blank. I did not have one single, solitary idea. The voice in my head started. *You can't think of any ideas because you haven't had a drink. You've never done a debate without a drink before. Remember how long it took you to do stand-up without a drink? Why on earth did you think you could do this sober? It's impossible. You can't do it.* Oh God, the voice made sense to me in the moment. And as we all know, as soon as I engage with the voice in my head, I lose.

At rehab, they taught us that relapsing with knowledge is dangerous and painful. At that stage of my addiction, my alcohol tolerance was extraordinarily high. I no longer experienced the luxurious relief you get when the second champagne hits you at a party. It would take so much alcohol to give me that feeling, that by the time I got there, I was behaving like the last person at the party, dancing on their own in the corner at 4 am. There was no tipsy; I went straight to blackout. While I was sober, my addiction had been doing push-ups in the corner, waiting for me to slip up so it could knock the lights out of me.

Walking down Collins Street, I stopped into a bottle shop to buy vodka. Two blocks later, I stopped into another bottle shop. I no longer had the ability to stop at my pre-show ritual of two mini bottles of Smirnoff. The first swallow was like lighting a campfire that spread so fast it raged out of control. By the time I got to the debate, I was legless. I made such a shameful fool of myself. Apparently. I have no recollection of the entire night, except for a single flash of memory of a town hall stage and lectern. It goes without saying, I lost the debate.

After the catastrophic event, I went on to cause havoc in Ballarat. The next day, Lawrence informed me that I was on the prowl in the dead of night looking for alcohol in my hotel. I rang room service and they told me they didn't sell alcohol after midnight. Undeterred, I went down to the front desk and told them that my girlfriend and I had just got engaged – same-sex marriage hadn't yet been legalised in Australia but I wasn't going to let that stop me – and asked for a bottle of champagne to celebrate. Yes! I capitalised on the back of the gay rights movement to get my alcohol fix. It was pure junkie behaviour.

The next day, Tess came to collect me from Ballarat. She was working as my PA at the time. Can you imagine her heartbreak, picking up her drunk mum just months after I'd got out of rehab? I think all hope was gone for her in that moment. I put myself straight into a private hospital when I arrived back in Melbourne. I wanted to douse the raging fire with an air tanker and put out the flames before they could burn any more.

*

While my debating skills were at an all-time low after rehab, my stand-up was better than ever. The upside to working my arse off to clear my tax debt (and pay my rent) was polishing my instrument. The best thing for a comedian's craft is an audience. Getting up on stage night after night kept me sharp and shiny. And doing it sober made me realise how hampered I had been. I can't watch videos of myself on YouTube pre-2014.

The difference between my drunk and sober performances was clear to me – and the audience. In 2015, a reviewer described my Melbourne International Comedy Festival show 'The One Where She Left Her Husband and Moved to Melbourne' as 'like a late-night bitch session with your hilarious aunt, rather than a traditional stand-up show'.

'After a public battle with alcoholism, marriage breakdown and a suicide attempt, she has risen again on stage like the Lady Lazarus of comedy. And yes she performs just as well – if not better now – being off the grog,' the review continued.

By mid-2017, my stand-up was sparkling and I was being offered headline shows, when I got the call to be a contestant on the fourth season of *I'm a Celebrity ... Get Me Out of Here!* Before my coma – and subsequent unravelling – I was meant to appear on *I'm a Celebrity*, I had my travel injections and was ready to go. Thank God I didn't make it. I imagine the only thing worse than unravelling in your cousin's bathtub fully clothed is unravelling on national TV halfway around the world in the middle of South Africa's Kruger National Park surrounded by cameras and other celebs.

When I got the offer, it felt like a second chance. It was as though I'd got out of rehab and things were finally looking up for me. Even if I only lasted two weeks, my fee would be $120 000, and if I made it to the final week, that would increase to $150 000. Finally, I was going to get the pay day I needed – and the financial security I craved. It wasn't just about the paycheque, though; there was another potential pot of gold at the end of the jungle rainbow. My friend Joel Creasey had been on the first season of the show and he told me it was going to do wonders for my career – and my ticket sales. After his stint on *I'm a Celebrity*, Joel went on to incredible success. I knew that going into the jungle would open doors I had never seen before and I was chomping at the bit to walk through those archways and slam the past behind me.

Plus, I was excited about who the other celebs might be – I knew that comedian Peter Rowsthorn of *Kath & Kim* fame had been cast and I was glad to know that someone like-minded would be in the jungle with me. There was also a rumour that Rob Lowe was going to be the token American celeb. Rob Lowe, to me, is the most perfect human being God ever created. Like, I get what he was doing with Brad Pitt, I get it. But he really nailed it with Rob Lowe.

As much as I wanted to bask in the glory of my redemption and the idea of living out my Rob Lowe fantasy, I had more pressing issues on my mind. I'm a huge arachnophobe and all I could think about were the spiders. I was also really worried about jumping out of a helicopter. Naturally. I couldn't see myself parachuting into the jungle surrounded by spiders, so I couldn't see the future opportunities either. It wasn't until I pulled the ripcord at 700 metres above ground and sailed through the steamy African air that it felt real.

When I landed in the camp, my groin was in excruciating pain from the parachute harness, but I was pleasantly surprised at the other contestants: singer Shannon Noll, model Simone Holtznagel, AFL player Josh Gibson, actress Kerry Armstrong, singer Tiffany Darwish, boxers Anthony Mundine and Danny Green, *Real Housewife of Melbourne* Jackie Gillies, and of course comedian Peter Rowsthorn, who became my 'camp husband'.

Peter and I assumed alter egos as Ron and Brenda and made ourselves laugh until it hurt. The producers introduced a segment called 'The Ron and Brenda Show', where we'd play our characters and do skits and have joke-offs. We even renewed our 'vows' one night. 'You, my dear Ron, are the antacid to my reflux,' I said, wearing a ceremonial flower crown, looking up at Ron. 'I come from a long line of short people, and I recall my tiny, tiny father saying to me with a tear in his eye, "He's the herd improver we've all been praying for."'

Ron and Brenda had a morbidly obese daughter called Kylie and a heavily pierced son called Dean, with huge holes in his ears that could fit a can of VB. 'He's having difficulty finding a job,' we joked.

'I'm worried about the kids. I hope Kylie's lap-band surgery went okay. She's a big girl, she gets it from your mother,' I said to Ron. 'She needs to lose weight or Gavin will leave her.'

'So, Brenda and Ron just appeared, Ron in the shape of Peter Rowsthorn and Brenda in me,' I explained in the confessional hut. 'It's almost like having a bit of a family of your own in here.'

In one segment called 'Ron and Brenda on the rocks', I sat on Danny Green's lap and Ron said, 'Oh Brenda, get your hands off him.'

'Oh, shut up, Ron,' I replied.

'She seems to have moved on with Danny Green with minimum fuss, looking at him luringly with those luring eyes of hers, often bra-less, which isn't great for everybody,' Ron explained in the confessional hut. We thought we were hilarious, and so did the rest of Australia, it appeared.

My first night in the jungle, sleeping on a camp bed under the South African stars with the sounds of monkeys and insects in the air, was surreal. The camp looked like something straight out of a postcard, and the jungle noises sounded like a pre-recorded tape of 'African Atmospheric Sounds'.

For the first three days in the jungle, I was nominated to do every challenge, where we competed to earn food for the camp. When they told me on the third day that I was doing the tucker-trial eating challenge with Jackie, Simone and Josh, I rolled around on the ground in the foetal position. When we got to 'The Grossery Store', Jackie had to eat raw impala brain; Simone had to eat cockroaches, mealworms and critters; and Josh had to eat an ostrich anus. I gagged watching him chew the anus. I was served a 'crocolate shake', which was blended crocodile, fish guts and sour Amasi (fermented milk). I downed it in one go, holding my breath to block out the taste.

In the second round, Josh and I were served a plate of poached bull testicles to share. As I lifted the ball sack to my mouth, a long-forgotten memory came into my mind. It was the voice of my Year 12 biology teacher Mr Lugg as he said in his South African accent, 'The vas deferens,' which is – of course – the correct terminology for the tube that transports sperm from the testicles to the urethra. The vas deferens was served on Josh's plate, so he drew the short straw and had to eat it. 'You know that I've loved you in this camp, so this is me showing how much I love you,' he told me as he put the sperm tube in his mouth. He vomited it back up less than a minute later. My hero.

Out of everyone, Jackie did my head in, but that's part of the show, we're all there to get on each other's nerves. Tension makes great TV. Compared to five months in rehab, the jungle was a breeze. I actually found it quite luxurious – well, not eating eyeballs or living in constant fear of tarantulas, but I enjoyed lounging around my camp bed chatting to Peter. There was a lot of sitting around. If we had a TV, I would have been in heaven.

The show is how it appears on TV. We didn't have producers slipping us caramel Tim Tams or make-up artists keeping us fresh faced. We only had physical interactions with the crew when we had to leave camp to undertake a challenge. Even then, we were blindfolded and taken to the site, and the producers hid their watches and the clocks so we never knew what time it was. We weren't given any feedback from the outside world and had no idea how we were coming across back in Australia. The director only came into camp once to give us a talking to, telling us, 'We need more stories.' Luckily, I had plenty of them.

Getting a message from home in the jungle after weeks away was almost as thrilling as getting a letter in rehab. I received a heartfelt note from Tess, which was read out by Paul Burrell, the royal butler who had come into the camp late. '*Dear*

Noni,' Tess wrote, '*I miss you. Not being able to contact you has made me realise how much I would have struggled had we lost you almost three years ago. You are the strongest woman I know, and I wouldn't change you for the world.'* I sobbed on national TV. Before I went into the jungle, Tess had told me she was pregnant, but she was so early we didn't know what would happen. When she called me Noni, I knew the baby was okay and she'd made it through the first trimester. Then they pulled out a TV screen and I got to see the first ultrasound of the baby on the show. Hearing that heartbeat was such a relief and a thrill. I slept with Tess's letter under my pillow that night. I thought back to my breakdown in rehab when I heard the voice of my future grandchild saying, 'Noni, I need you.' If only they knew how much I needed them, too.

*

When English celebrity Vicky Pattison came into the jungle after almost three weeks, she told me on the sly that I was by far the frontrunner in the competition. She had won the UK version in 2015, and she told me how life-changing it would be for me. I freaked out. Suddenly, I felt the scrutiny of millions of eyes on me. I started having some wild panic attacks. I would replay every conversation I'd had in the jungle over and over. I had opened up to Peter about my life and struggles – I spoke about my alcoholism, about Mary-Agnes saving me from my suicide attempt, about the depths of my desperation and my most hideous relapse – and I had a terrible fear that my candid conversations would bite me on the arse.

After six weeks in the jungle, the situation started messing with my head; I spoke very freely and almost forgot the cameras were there. I had delusions that I was the schmuck. I thought that the reason I hadn't been voted off yet was because I was the butt of the joke. I could almost hear all of Australia laughing at me from South Africa.

In the middle of a paranoid freakout, I went to the long drop in the dead of night and drank hand sanitiser. It was an absurd and desperate thing to do. For the risk I took, the payoff was awful. Drinking hand sanitiser is not like drinking alcohol, I didn't get a buzz or relief; it just put me straight to sleep. It was half an hour of dry retching for a moment of numbness. I couldn't get the taste out of my mouth.

I wish I could tell you I only did this once, but that is not the case.

By the time I got to the final five, though, it started to feel like all roads were actually heading somewhere wonderful.

Hell, maybe Vicky was right, maybe I was the favourite. Naturally, I had to self-sabotage. The voice in my mind got louder and louder. *You don't deserve this*, it said. *Who are you trying to kid?* And, unfortunately, I listened. The voice always wins. Hand sanitiser did not dull that voice.

On the second-last day, when the competition was down to me, Vicky, Danny and Shannon, I was walking out of camp and saw my sister Cate and son Bert standing on the wooden bridge that led to the swimming hole. I thought they were a mirage at first, but then I squealed and ran and hugged them tight. When Bert said, 'You're doing so well, Mum,' I nearly burst with pride.

'How have I been looking on TV, Cate?' I asked.

'Oh, I haven't been watching because I'm not in it. I'll watch this episode because I'm in it,' she joked. God, I had missed her.

Later, to the camera, I said, 'Over the six weeks that I've been here, it's all down to your loved ones at the end of the day. That's what rolls over and over in your mind like a tape.'

That night sitting around the campfire with my remaining camp mates and their family members, I sang 'Danny Boy' with Bert playing the guitar and singing back-up. I think even big, tough Danny Green had a little cry.

*

When I woke up on the day of the finale, I vowed to savour every minute. You only have a few really big days in your life, and I knew this was going to be one of them. I wasn't worried about winning or losing, because I felt like I'd already won – as clichéd as that might sound. On the way to the grand finale ceremony, I was sitting on the back of a motorbike driven by one of the producers when she crashed into a tree. Neither of us was hurt and the bike was okay, so we just got back on and kept going. I didn't know whether we were unlucky because we crashed, or lucky because we weren't injured. Either way, I'd stopped believing in talismans when I performed sober for the first time without my rabbit's foot vodka.

When it came down to me and Shannon Noll as the final two, the hosts Dr Chris Brown and Julia Morris stood in front of us. I'd known Julia for twenty years and we'd had some wonderful boozy nights together before I got on the wagon. She's funny all the way in and out. Every time she came into camp during filming, it was like having a relative visit me in school while I tried to pretend I didn't know them. When Julia held the winning envelope, I had an overwhelming knowledge that my name was on the card. No offence to Shannon, but I knew I had it over him.

When Julia read out my name, all I felt was relief. As they placed the Jungle Queen crown on my head, I thought, *I've put everything right as best I can.* This was about more than a reality show for me, it was about doing my family proud, righting my wrongs and proving I was worthy. Part of me was thrilled to know that people actually liked me. When I found out I had won with 63 per cent of the votes, it was so affirming. Plus, I'd won $100 000 prize money for my selected charity Angel Flight.

The local South Australian paper *The Advertiser* ran a photo of Mum and Dad celebrating my win at the front bar of the Warooka Hotel holding champagne flutes in the air. They looked so happy and proud to be my parents. I was glad I was sober, because I could feel the pure joy of the moment. A sense of peace soaked all the way into my bones. I felt exonerated, and I released the guilt and shame I'd been carrying.

Wearing my crown and sitting on my throne, I thanked everyone for their support. 'I think I'll be laughing until I'm eighty. And that's not far away from the way I'm feeling today. I'm so tired and yet so happy. My first duty as Jungle Queen is to deal with my hygiene. I hope to be carted around in this chair by my minions looking very regal. I did not think six weeks ago that I would be here sitting in this chair – bloody hell, I just won *I'm a Celebrity*,' I joked. My ship had come in and I was taking my seat in the captain's chair.

The night of the finale, the rest of the cast and crew went out for a big night on the town to celebrate, and I went to dinner with Bert and Cate and had a long hot bath in my hotel room.

In my final piece to camera on *I'm a Celebrity*, I said, 'I'm not leaving [the jungle], I've got nowhere to go.' It was a joke, with a hint of truth. My favourite kind.

CHAPTER 11

DEAFENING SILENCE

AT JOHANNESBURG AIRPORT ON MY WAY BACK TO Australia, I ran into one of the Channel 10 producers. His excitement for me gushed out. He said, 'I really think you showed us you can do everything. You've made us laugh and cry, and you listen to people. I think you're the only talent in Australia who could give us our own Graham Norton talk show.' I spent the entire flight back to Melbourne dreaming about being Australia's answer to Graham Norton and thinking about potential names for my talk show … *On the Couch with Fiona O'Loughlin* had a terrible ring to it but I had to start somewhere.

Within hours of winning, I was in a production meeting with the senior team at Channel 10. They asked me what kind of show I wanted to make, and I pitched a few ideas. One of them was a Ron and Brenda sitcom. Another was a reality-TV-flipping-houses-type show, renovating our family's old farmhouse, Cletta, with my sisters, including Emily who is one of the best, if not *the* best, comedic actress in the country. We would talk up and down ladders while we renovated the house our great-grandfather built when he came out from Ireland. It would be a cross between *The Real Housewives of Adelaide*, *Fixer Upper* and *Who Do You Think You Are?*. While we hilariously renovated the house, we'd have deep conversations about our childhood, family history and memories of growing up in the sixties. I knew people liked seeing me in a reality setting and they enjoyed my candid stories; plus, renovation shows were all the rage, so I assumed this idea would be a given. I'd done my job and proved I was popular and watchable, they just had to give me the screen time.

I started living like the Queen I was crowned. I treated myself to a tummy tuck to get rid of my five-babies-belly and the excess skin I had after losing 10 kilograms in the jungle. After five caesareans, the surgery felt like a routine Tuesday hospital appointment, and they gave me codeine for the recovery, so I was sorted.

I rented a beautiful house in Melbourne and waited for the phone to ring. I knew someone was going to call and give me the big break that would set me up for life. Every time my phone buzzed, I jumped with anticipation. All I wanted was for my kids to see me in a house of my own, so they never had to worry about their mum sleeping rough again.

Thinking I was about to get a reality TV series with my sisters any minute, I started the 'My Dear Sister Catherine' letter series with Cate in mid-2018. We traded veiled insults and witty prose in correspondence. These letters followed on from my early rendition on stage of a letter I actually wrote to Cate in response to Chris suggesting I put pen to paper 'like the pioneer women would have done' all those years ago.

My Dear Sister Catherine,

I hope you are enjoying this long weekend with your large family. Please remember that I am recovering from an abdominal 'procedure' so I shan't be receiving calls until I meet again with my acclaimed Melbourne surgeon mid-week.

However, my personal assistant has been reorganising my clothing wardrobe and since I will no longer be requiring my firming undergarments I wondered if they would be of use to you? I have no doubt that your nine natural births have wreaked havoc on your own midriff (not to mention the 'arena' downstairs) and with the marching of time it must be irresistible for you to deny yourself of any support I am able to generously provide.

My daughter Tessie will arrange the postage of my now redundant underthings, as my rising profile inhibits me markedly in public places such as the Post Office. I never thought I'd say this but I find myself envious of your social positioning from time to time.

How splendid for you to live in such abject anonymity. But I have no complaints, dear. Life is a wonderful experience for me at the moment. Who would have thought that I would end up with the flatter tummy between the pair of us? Oh heavens! It's almost as if I can hear your delighted giggles of happiness for me from here!!!

I look forward to hearing from you. There is no need to thank me for this uplifting post. I live by the code that if a day has not included enhancing another's, then that is indeed a day wasted.

Lovingly yours,

Fiona xx

My Dear Sister Fiona,

How marvellous to hear from you after all this time! I was beginning to think you'd been sent to darkest Africa? Uncanny that I would hear from you when I myself have just returned from the local Postal Office.

Of course I have no reason to fear recognition in this small community as my reputation is held in the highest regard, given that I am married to the local veterinarian and as a regular churchgoer am often seen volunteering my time to various charities.

I can only hope that the hand-knitted garments for the orphans of Uzbekistan and the emergency parcels for the survivors of the volcanic eruption in Guatemala have made it safely to those in need! Here I am chattering on about my good deeds to the needy while you, my poor dear, languish in bed recovering from a 'tummy tuck'!!! How splendid, and at your age?

I did so pity you for having to carry that gross encumbrance around your midriff for so many years and to perform on stage, night after night, as if it was of no handicap at all? Funny that you still blame your sizeable girth on the bearing of five children when your dearest and closest sister had almost double that number and with each pregnancy bounced back as slim and svelte as she was before! Perhaps proof that there is merit in a more disciplined approach to diet and exercise postnatally, thus preventing the inevitable extreme of going under the surgeon's knife? Wonderful that we live in such a medically advanced society whereby a team of specialist surgeons can be put together for such an epic procedure on one overfed tummy!

Do be careful, dear, for as you know comedy greats such as Phyllis Diller and Joan Rivers went a little 'too far' in the alteration of their appearance and if you were to emulate them in your unbridled quest for fame and fortune, then we shall all be 'rolling in the aisles' – so to speak!!!!

Fondest love,

Catherine

My Dear Sister Catherine,

Before I even begin to tell you of the struggles I have endured these past twenty-four hours, please know that my emotions are running wild and I am in an extreme state of irritation. You will need to allow me licence to be brisk in tone and clipped in content as I want to expedite the release of my tension and ask that your own domestic diatribes be put aside for this moment in time. Television's night of nights was a disappointment of great magnitude.

My travails commenced in the wardrobe department. As you are well aware, unlike yourself, I have never been an attendant to vanity thereby you of all people can envision my distress. Upon arriving at the grand ballroom of The Star on the Gold Coast where the designer frocks hung splendidly in readiness to adorn the many female luminaries under the banner of Network Ten, the very worst had transpired, Catherine. My gown was as near identical as one could conceive to that of a young Queensland newsreader.

Though you well know that I have kindness of heart that would rival a deceased Bride of Christ known primarily for her work in Calcutta (God rest her soul), but even Mother Teresa herself must have had her patience tested from time to time. I hope this flabbergasts you as it did me that it was suggested that I should be the one to resort to wearing a 'back-up' gown! Can you imagine? I made a steely resolve to not negotiate further as I believed my sufferings in the African Jungle had more than equipped me to maintain my standpoint that I indeed outranked my regional rival.

I'm pleased to say that I was victorious in claiming the adornment of my satin emerald green garment as you may well have witnessed on the live television broadcast as I presented myself on the red carpet. What should have been a triumphant

moment, however, was somewhat spoiled by the lasting
recollection of some very raised eyebrows at my determination in
the dressing room.

When I lay back into the luxury of all the ostentatious
pillowing my high-end hotel bed had to offer, post-ceremony,
I used the Google application on my telecommunication device
to assuredly delight in my appearance on the best dressed menu
in the first notification I could find.

I have never thrown a telephone across a room before,
Catherine, but in this instance I could see no alternative to
medicate my utter disappointment.

Yours lovingly forever,

Fiona

Dearest Fiona,

I have set aside my secateurs and sun hat (having just
commenced some pruning of my vast rose garden) to reply to the
rather fractious letter I have just received and hope, dearest, that
my most considerate ear can avail you of some respite from your
despair! Poor dear, it seems that you have indeed had the 'night
of nights' starting with your emerald green gown.

I can only imagine the conniption that ensued when you
discovered a more youthful, possibly 'prettier' commercial

network celebrity had intentions of wearing the very same frock!
I'm sure the entire dressing room was ducking for cover when
the ferocity of your ire reached its peak (I of all people know
what is to be on the receiving end of one of your verbal tirades
regarding an article of clothing that you deem to be yours!).

Still, as the old idiom goes, 'Age before beauty.'

I had a dreadful vision of your little reality show winning
its genre and of you, my dear, bulldozing your way towards
the podium in your rambunctious manner, knocking people
sideways in your quest to get your greedy hands on the 'prize'.
Alas! This was not your year. Tell me, dearest, is there a reality
show you have yet to take part in???

I must fly, as my Book Club group awaits. Funny, we've
been revisiting the classics and this apt quote from Emily
Dickinson came to mind, 'Fame is a fickle food upon a shifting
plate.' Careful what you eat, dear sister.

Yours with my affection,

Catherine

At TV's aforementioned 'night of nights', the Logies in July 2018, I ran into one of the hosts from the morning show *Studio 10* wearing my emerald green gown and Stuart Weitzman heels. The host told me Denise Drysdale was leaving the show and that I was up for the job. I was friends with Denise and she'd hinted at the same thing. Morning TV would have been the last choice on my list of dream jobs, but I still would have done it. I figured, it would have been a regular paycheque with sick leave and superannuation. I thought I could do it for five years, keep gigging and start saving for retirement.

I turned on the TV a few weeks later and saw them announce Kerri-Anne Kennerley as the new *Studio 10* host.

Not to worry, I had heard whispers the Nine Network were bringing back *Australia's Got Talent*, and I could picture myself sitting on the judges' panel next to Kyle Sandilands and Dannii Minogue wearing a splendid sequin number. The franchise was owned by Simon Cowell, whose talent-show judging panel always included a funny older lady such as Dawn French or Sharon Osbourne. I thought, *I want that job*. I told my agent to go hard. He hounded them for a meeting, only to be told I didn't have enough experience for the role. I'd only been selling out stand-up shows for two decades and had just won the biggest reality TV show in the country. Plus, I was an expert at judging people from my couch. What more experience could they want? I was furious, but mostly disappointed.

With *AGT* off the table, I thought at the very least I would get an endorsement ad. I'd done a series of ads for Heinz soup back in the day and was paid $78 000. I thought everyone who appeared on a reality TV show in Australia automatically got a teeth-whitening gig. I was wrong. I started to feel sick waiting for the phone to ring.

*

One day the phone did ring, but not about endorsements or TV shows. It was the best news: Tess was in labour. I rushed to the hospital to be with her, but I had a plane to catch and a gig to do interstate, so I had to leave before my grandchild was born. Úna Mary came into the world fifteen minutes later. A picture of her little face appeared on my phone in the car on the way to the airport. She was everything I'd hoped for and more. I had dreamed of becoming a Noni since I was a teenage babysitter, and even more so after my vision in rehab. When I held tiny Úna in my arms three days later, I felt like a matriarch. It was a rush like no other. It's different from having your own child, but every bit as powerful.

I knew Tess would be a natural mother, and she bloody is. Watching my daughter become a mother was extraordinary.

As a grandma, all I had to do was be Úna's soft place to land. I could be the good guy in her story. It was delicious knowing I couldn't let her down, I could just enjoy her.

Úna has brought us all closer together. My kids are besotted with her, Bert even wrote her a song ...

A Letter to Úna

Úna Mary, one day you're gonna dance with me,
One day you're gonna cry with me.
Úna Mary, one day you're gonna mourn with me;
You're gonna have to say goodbye with me.
Úna Mary, well, then I'll ask you to sing for me,
'Oh, Úna, won't you sing for me?'
Úna Mary, I know you're gonna grow old too,
And I know that someone will want to marry you.
And Úna Mary, how long before you can walk with me?
And will you ever confide in me?
Úna Mary, one day you're gonna dance with me,
'Oh, Úna, won't you dance with me?'

We wet the baby's head in a beautiful ceremony at our house in Melbourne. Ciarán's father came out from Ireland, my mum and dad came up from Warooka and all my kids were there.

People travelled thousands of kilometres to hover around this baby. And she was so worth the journey. It was a joyous night, ending with Bert's precious song.

The next morning, I caught a flight to Paris with Mum, Dad and Bert. I took my parents to Paris because I wanted to say sorry. It was a guilt trip, literally. I just wanted to make some good memories together, and we did.

Walking the streets of the city of love with my parents was surreal – and not very romantic. There's a great picture of Dad and me wearing berets and looking like total tourists. I look genuinely happy in the photo, and I was. I felt relieved the whole holiday, as though I were paying my dues and making things right. I was the Jungle Queen and I had taken my parents on the trip of a lifetime; surely all was forgiven? I bent over backwards to make sure everyone had the best time. Mum has always liked my hair short, so one day I walked across the road to a hairdresser and got all of my hair chopped off just to make her happy (and promptly let it grow back again when I returned to Melbourne).

*

When I returned from Paris, my ears stung with deafening silence, for the umpteenth time in my life. It was a familiar sound, but I hadn't heard it coming. I was sure the phone was going to ring with a big TV offer, but it didn't. After all the years I spent sitting tight-lipped at home, I was used to silence. It was good training. And after rehab, I was in much better shape mentally and felt equipped to handle the suffocating disappointment.

By the time I gave up staring at my phone willing it to vibrate, I started to worry about my financial situation and called my close friend Sue who had nursed me back to health in Adelaide, asking her to come to Melbourne to go over my books with me. I wanted to take back control. Sue had owned various businesses over a number of years and knew how to read a spreadsheet. She found a confusing letter from the tax office stuffed in a drawer and got on the phone to them straightaway to try and make sense of it. Thank God she did, because they told her I was about to be sent a notice that I was being garnisheed by the tax office. They were going to empty my bank accounts without any warning. Sue managed to negotiate a payment arrangement so that didn't happen. I owed them another $103 000. Sue officially took over as my bookkeeper.

*

I still don't know why I didn't receive any offers after *I'm a Celebrity*. Maybe I had pissed off someone in power, or maybe my past behaviour had finally caught up with me. Apart from the disaster in New Zealand, I hadn't been drunk on screen since my early *Good News Week* appearances, but I felt like I'd been blacklisted from the mainstream channels for my reputation. On the street and in Facebook messages, I was asked why I never appeared on various prime-time panel shows. It was awkward and humiliating – and I truly didn't know the answer.

My friend Tom Gleeson had me on his show *Hard Chat*. 'Are you jealous of high-functioning alcoholics like myself?' he asked. ''Cause I can sink a lot of piss and still earn a living, that must really shit you.'

'Yes, it does,' I said, cackling.

Something else that shit me was finding out footballer Brendan Fevola had been paid $350 000 when he won *I'm a Celebrity* in 2016 and cricketer Shane Warne had negotiated a $2 million salary for his appearance the same year – compared to my $150 000 paycheque. I had never experienced sexism in the stand-up scene, but I certainly felt I was judged more harshly for being an alcoholic than my male peers. Some of the best male comics have battled with addiction, but it's never mentioned in a negative way. I never saw a 'bad boy' at the top of their game get rejected because of their disease. Men are often spun as 'having demons', but the word 'alcoholic' is rarely said out loud, so they can keep drinking beer in public. Calling it what it really is would be too scary, make them too vulnerable, be too honest. We all have demons, but not everyone drinks themself to death over them. Demons don't kill alcoholics. Alcohol kills alcoholics.

I was in rehab when radio host and self-confessed alcoholic Derryn Hinch was photographed drinking wine. Now, it's none of my business what Derryn puts in his mouth, but his blasé reaction to drinking made me boil. In 2011, he had had a lifesaving liver transplant because his was lethally damaged by his alcoholism.

Derryn defended his actions by saying, 'I swore I would never drink again, but you have got to live your life.' He claimed that his doctor had given the all-clear to have a few drinks, admitting, 'I have a couple of glasses of wine a couple of times a week.' No doctor in their right mind would give an alcoholic the all-clear to have a few drinks. When Derryn made that ridiculous claim, he gave false hope to alcoholics everywhere. We all dream of being able to drink normally and having the power to stop after a couple of beers, but we cannot.

Alcohol kills alcoholics. I don't judge Derryn for relapsing, but I do think he may have endangered others by his claim.

*

I gave up waiting for the phone to ring and hit the road with Peter Rowsthorn for a regional tour of 'Ron and Brenda Go Country'. We booked in dates at Caboolture RSL in Queensland, Red Earth Arts Precinct in Karratha, Western Australia, Bunjil Place Theatre in Victoria and every civic centre, town hall and country club in between. Our tagline was:

> What happened in the jungle, stays in the jungle ... or so everybody thought until 'Ron and Brenda Go Country'. The official 'Jungle Queen', Fiona O'Loughlin, and her unofficial King, Peter Rowsthorn, escaped the Channel 10 celebrity torture fest and have headed to the relative safety of stand-up comedy to share their stories on life, the world and the making of reality TV.

We spent zero time planning our routine. We knew we'd each get up and do thirty minutes of our stand-up and then come together as Ron and Brenda and dish on secrets from behind the scenes of *I'm a Celebrity*, but that was as far as our planning had gone. Two weeks before our first show, I called Peter worried about our lack of preparation. 'What are we going to do?' I asked. 'What is the show going to *be*?'

'Fiona, it doesn't matter,' he reassured me. 'These people are buying tickets to see two half-baked characters from a reality TV show. It doesn't matter what we do.' He was right. Ron and Brenda had a cult following and their fans lapped up the live show. We killed it every night. On social media, they were calling for Channel 10 to produce a Ron and Brenda sitcom, and obviously that didn't happen, so this was the next best thing.

Peter is saved in my phone as 'Ron' and our text conversations are often in character ...

Ron: Happy New Year, Brenda. Spotlight's out of control today. Won't be home before midnight.

Ron: I made a gorgeous halter-neck top for you yesterday. It's in the cupboard. Surprise!!!

Brenda: You do spoil me, Ron. Sorry about all the yelling this morning. Kylie unlocked the fridge again during the night and she's polished off the cheese platter I had ready for this evening. I hope she chokes on a Kabana skin. Did you want me to tape the fireworks and we'll watch it in the morning?

Ron: Morning, Brenda, are you up and about? I saw a wool shop that had lots of half balls of yarn at out-they-go prices for some Xmas gifts I'm making. Would you like to join me? Fair chance they'll have some old patterns lying around as well.

Brenda: Hello Ron. The wool shop sounds intriguing. Actually, it sounds horrific and boring. When will we head off?

Ron: What about a five-and-a-half-hour drive, then? I'm good to go now.

Ron: Got your game face on, Brenda?

It's me Ron.

Brenda: Hey RON!!!!!!!!!

Where are you staying?

Ron: At Kylie's!!! The menu 🍔🍔🍔🍔🍔🍔🍔🍔🍔🍔

How are you getting to Ringwood?

For God's sake, Brenda?

Brenda: Uber at 8.

On 26 October 2019, we took Ron and Brenda to where it all started for me: Warooka. The locals swept the wooden floor of the Warooka Town Hall and brought in extra chairs in anticipation for the show. We filled the hall. I felt like the prodigal daughter returning home in a blaze of glory as the Jungle Queen, and Warooka welcomed me back with open arms and belly laughs.

The after party was held at Mum and Dad's place, naturally. I felt like a teenager again, heading back to our family kitchen table after last call at the Warooka Hotel. More than forty years later, Mum and Dad could still pull a crowd. The kitchen table felt smaller than ever, cramped with locals and flowing with beer and wine. I stood there for a moment, without a glass in my hand, and drank up the gratitude. It might not have been the kitchen table I dreamed of as a little girl watching American sitcoms, but it was a testament to a much bigger story. This house touched so many and everyone was welcome – especially if you had a good tale to tell and a six-pack under your arm.

Mum and Dad stayed up with the crowd until 3 am. I had to leave. Once the adrenaline of the show wore off, I took myself back to my accommodation in town and away from the free-flowing booze and the party hards. I chose to look after myself instead of waiting around to be tempted – how very mature of me; it only took fifty-six years to learn my lesson.

I wasn't sad about leaving the party early, I was at peace with the knowledge that for me, that party was over.

*

I moved back to Adelaide towards the end of 2019 and asked Sue to take over as my manager. I'd seen a direct correlation between my friendship with Sue and my mental wellbeing. The more we worked together, the easier and better everything became. I didn't just need a personal assistant, I needed a partner, a friend, a support person. I said out loud, 'I need help.' And she helped me. Sue had met me at my lowest and had seen how hard I fought to stay alive. I finally had someone in my life with whom I could be completely honest. While I've always had my family around me, I felt like I couldn't turn to them when I was having a rough day – I'd put them through too much already, they didn't need to hear me whingeing about my worries. With Sue backing me up, I felt freer to struggle and thereby safer to be honest. For all the years I sat in AA meetings, there was a poster hanging on the wall that said, 'Only I can do this, but I cannot do it alone.' Truer words were never written on an inspirational poster.

With Sue's help, I put my disease at the forefront of everything I did. If I had a bad feeling about a gig, she encouraged me to turn it down. If I needed a day off, I'd take it and spend the day in bed watching *Real Housewives*. It was as though I had finally stumbled across the answer I'd been looking for, searching for, praying for. And it came in the form of a friend, an ally, and finding someone with a mutual understanding of addiction and mental illness.

I don't think even I can fully appreciate the energy it took for my children to stay hopeful and recharge again and again after every relapse. Especially Tess, who became the family-appointed go to in regard to all my incidents and hospitalisations all the while working as my PA. By hell, I owe that girl a lot.

CHAPTER 12

IS THE END
IN SIGHT?

I REMEMBER THE EXACT MOMENT I WAS INTRODUCED TO the allure of codeine. I was in a recovery meeting in 2009, going through the motions, checking in with the group to see how long it had been between drinks for everyone. One of my good friends spoke up. 'Well, I'm not drinking, but I am doing something else and I have been for a while. I don't want to say what it is,' she revealed. My ears pricked. She had been taking Panadeine Extra to fill the numbing void of alcohol. Because that's what addiction is all about: an endless quest for relief, a dulling of pain, a moment of unfeeling. The revelation planted a seed in my head, I kept Panadeine Extra in the back of my mind as a stopgap for drinking, should I ever need it.

I pulled out the crumpled note from the back of my mind in 2018 when I was blindsided by the deafening silence I heard after winning *I'm a Celebrity*. Instead of drinking, I started taking codeine. If I wanted to bliss out and watch Netflix for twelve hours straight, I would pop a few pills. If I had to go to a birthday party or a wedding or any social event where there would be alcohol, I would pop a few pills. If I had to be on my game and put on my happy/funny/sober Fiona face, I would pop a few pills. The buzz from codeine was different from alcohol. They both numbed the pain, but the feeling after swallowing a handful of tablets was euphoric.

The most I would take in a 24-hour period was ten to twelve, taking five or six of them in one go. I was careful not to overdo it, but more careful about rationing my limited supply. The government introduced laws in early 2018 that meant people needed to have a prescription from a doctor to buy codeine medication; you could no longer get it over the counter at a pharmacy for a 'toothache'. It sure made having an opioid addiction hard. Luckily, I had prescriptions from my tummy tuck, but I knew they wouldn't last forever. Every time I visited the home of a friend or relative, I would make an excuse to use their bathroom and go through their drawers looking for Panadeine Extra. I stole tablets from my mum and dad. I told myself it was better than drinking.

I could feel myself slipping down another addictive slide – but this time I wasn't going down without a fight. I grabbed onto the railing of the slippery dip and pulled myself up. Nothing disastrous had happened like it had when I was an alcoholic, but I knew I had a problem and I needed help. I didn't want to hide away in another drug den, I wanted to face it. I felt like I'd already lost enough to addiction. I missed my eldest son's thirtieth birthday because I was in rehab. I squandered job opportunities because of my unreliability. I gave up any chance of having the financial security I worked all my life for. I lost time, wallets, entire weekends, friends, my sense of self, a bit of respect and a few brain cells.

One night I was Googling ways to hypnotise myself to fall asleep without codeine and came across the writings of Wayne Dyer, an American self-help guru who lives as a Dao. One verse quoting Lao Tzu hit me between the eyes: 'Only when we are sick of our sickness shall we cease to be sick.' I was sick to death of my addictive bullshit.

Daoism is a Chinese philosophical concept, similar to Buddhism. It's like a handbook on how to live – but not a preachy, fear-mongering one. Basically, it's spirituality for dummies. It's all about manifesting what you need, so I prayed to the universe for help with my codeine problem.

Two days later, Sue booked me in to see a doctor who specialises in addiction. When I told him about my issue, he explained how my codeine dependency was affecting my brain. He said, 'Ten per cent of Caucasian people cannot convert codeine to morphine. Thirty milligrams converts to two to three milligrams of morphine for pain relief, but it is as potent as morphine in increasing tolerance or cravings. So, it's ten times as addictive. Sadly, codeine will increase tolerance, even if it is not converted.' I was one of those people. When I first took fentanyl after my coma, the receptors in my brain were activated and started screaming for codeine from that moment. I was ready to go to rehab again to stop the screaming. I knew exactly what I was looking at and prepared myself to cancel the upcoming Adelaide Fringe show I'd booked. I was never going to be a bed partner with denial again.

Instead of shipping me off to a clinic, my doctor treated my addiction. First with medication and now with hypnotherapy and counselling. The voice in my head is silent all day everyday for the first time in my life. The medication blocks the receptors in my brain and negates any of the euphoria I would get from codeine. I no longer crave codeine, because it no longer has any effect on me. The same goes for booze. Now, I recoil from the thought of a drink, like a hand from a lit flame. It's not a struggle anymore. I refer to that doctor's appointment as 'the miracle', because even though I know there isn't an overnight cure for alcoholism, it was a miraculous moment for me. Later I asked Sue how she found the doctor and she told me the healer had recommended him. Maybe the healer did help save me after all.

Every morning now I wake up and say, 'How may I serve the world and myself today?' And the first thing on that list is: Don't relapse. That's my primary objective every day: Don't relapse. Don't take codeine. Don't have a drink. It's my job. And even though I'm still talking to an invisible God-like 'source', it feels a lot more comfortable than Catholicism ever did. At the end of each day, I reflect on my behaviours, examine my motives and check in on my conscience like my mother always taught us to do.

Through this process I have been able to let go of my guilt about turning my back on Catholicism. It would be unsafe for me to go to church now. I pray to my God easily ten times a day and have done so since I employed my sober coach, Robert, after my final relapse in 2019, who drummed it into me that prayer is as vital as exercise. Apart from the departed who I often talked to, like Chris's mum, Geraldine, and my deceased childhood cousin, Felicity, I had never given prayer a real go. I didn't know how to pray or to whom, nor what to say. But, my sober coach told me I could pray to the ocean for all he cared. Being an alcoholic in recovery himself, he swore it was the last missing element. I was forced to understand what my God is. I prayed to a holy spirit of universal energy. A big, fat, happy notion of tapping into all the love and kindness we have and sharing it with each other collectively. When I started praying, things started getting better at a rate of knots.

I still hold some resentment towards Catholicism and the shame it entrenched in me. Although my kids were baptised, we didn't go to Mass regularly and we certainly didn't read passages from the Bible as bedtime stories. I thought I had raised my kids fairly liberally; they were free to watch R-rated shows as teenagers and we all made crude jokes, but they still inherited my shame surrounding sex. I think my eldest daughter, Biddy, was especially affected by my silence on the issue. Of course, I didn't find that out until years later, because we never spoke about it. Silence breeds silence. I never told Biddy explicitly that I'd married her dad because we'd had sex before marriage and I didn't want to go to hell, but maybe she knew within herself when she looked at our wedding photos and saw me in my Kewpie-doll tulle dress, so young and naïve, desperate to 'do the right thing' by my family and God. I wish I could have broken the chain of silence locked by the Catholic Church before it had the chance to strangle my kids, but I didn't have the key and I wasn't strong enough to use bolt cutters.

In 2006, when Biddy turned eighteen, she packed up her life and moved to London. Chris and I happened to be in London because I was filming a comedy special, and she stayed with us in our hotel when she arrived. She dumped her suitcase in the corner and lay down beside me on the double bed; all she wanted to do was hold my hand. In the background played the Snow Patrol song 'Chasing Cars', about lying down and just forgetting the world. If only I had asked Biddy if she was okay. Or if she wanted to talk to me. Or why she was moving to a city on the other side of the world all on her own.

Unfortunately, I was drinking cranberry juice and vodka the day Biddy arrived, and I probably wouldn't have listened to her properly even if she had told me what was troubling her. If only I had been a mother who had English muffins for breakfast instead of Smirnoff. Years later, Biddy did tell me her story and my heart simultaneously broke for the young girl who couldn't turn to her mother for help, and swelled with pride for the woman she became all on her own.

*

In my years spent lounging on the couch, I've watched a lot of *Dr Phil* – mostly to mock him mercilessly and rubbish his ridiculous advice. But there's one thing he says in his Southern drawl that rings true: 'The best predictor of future behaviour is past behaviour.'

Even with my newfound spirituality and outlook, I know I'm susceptible to relapse. I've spent years researching my disease like a detective. I've listened to every podcast on alcoholism, read every report and book, gone to every bloody meeting and sought help from every doctor I could. With my investigative research and extensive first-hand knowledge, I developed my own safety plan. I decided to create my own 'rat heaven' and live like I was in rehab, at home. I made my little flat in Adelaide a safe haven, filled with nice belongings and surrounded by good people. I decided I would no longer put myself in any situation that threatened my sobriety. I wouldn't go to venues or events where there would be alcohol except for work. I would skip Christmas and boozy birthday parties. I would remove myself from temptation. I even took away my access to cash and credit cards in the early days and gave the responsibility to someone I trusted so I couldn't go to the bottle shop on a whim. Coming up with my safety plan felt like a thunderbolt moment. I was free.

My last sip of alcohol was in mid-December 2019 after a couple of bust outs earlier in the year. I found out that I had been offered a 6 pm slot at the Melbourne International Comedy Festival. Worse, the slot was at The Westin Hotel, which was being trialled as a venue for the first time. It was a kick in the teeth (and you know how triggering broken teeth are for me). I was a headline act, doing the best work of my career, and they'd given me an embarrassingly early gig in an unknown venue. I felt defeated. No matter how hard I tried, no matter how sober I was, no matter how many reality TV shows I won, I was never going to be good enough. I would never be able to make up for my past wrongs, so I may as well have another drink. Or so the voice in my head told me.

I was frightened by how quickly I went to blackout. My physical hangover was entwined with my mental hangover. I tried to lie as still as I could in the hospital bed I'd checked into. If I was still, I was okay. Waves of nausea hit me so hard I had to run to the toilet to vomit and shit. Sometimes at the same time. My throat burned with bile and my mind burned with flashes of memory of what I'd said and done the night before.

In the light of day, I kept my guilt alive by replaying my existence and my misgivings over and over again. I wasn't allowed to live without the guilt. Shame engulfed me like lava. I begged for sleep and longed for darkness. I spent two days in bed, not eating, just rocking back and forth to soothe myself. If I didn't have to work, I could easily sleep for two days after a relapse, shaking with withdrawals. I'd been in that bed many times before. Except, this time I knew I could be sober. I had learned so much at rehab and proved to myself that I could beat the monster inside me. I was disappointed in my own weakness, but I wasn't destroyed by it. It's a long climb out of relapse, but I'd hiked the mountain and knew the shortcuts like the back of my hand.

Leaving hospital after my last relapse was the first time I didn't collapse into a pit of self-pity and self-rebuke. I knew I had a safe place to recover, and I had Sue to rely on. In a weird way, I'm grateful to the healer because she brought me in contact with Sue. I wouldn't be where I am today had I not hit rock bottom in that drug den in Adelaide and fought for my life.

There was no anger or finger-pointing from Sue, so the least I could give her in return was to heal quickly by eating and getting back on track – and not wasting time rolling around in the mud with guilt. Dogs fucking bark, so be it.

Here's what I still find hard to understand. Alcoholism has been around since the dawn of time, and as long as there is alcohol there will always be alcoholics. Alcohol is first and foremost a drug, and a highly addictive one at that. We know like the sun comes up tomorrow that alcohol is deadly and destructive to about 10 per cent of the drinking population and here we are in 2020 and still our collective reasoning is that these 10 per cent of human beings are defective, weak, pathetic and somehow 'less than' the 90 per cent of the population who are able to drink with impunity. The shame and stigma surrounding alcoholism is crazily counterproductive, archaic and dangerous.

I see a future where every single child will learn in school about the inverse allergy. That alcohol is a legal drug that will be ruinous to 10 per cent of them. Alcohol was the gateway drug to everything for me. Of course, I am ashamed of my behaviours when I was intoxicated but I will never again feel shame for drawing that genetic short straw. Ever. As much as I agree with the making amends process of the 12 steps, there are only so many times one person can apologise.

At fifty-seven, I have shaken hands with the universe and said, 'That's it.' I'm done. I feel very much at peace. I've learned that the most important moment of my life is right now and the most important person in my life is the person standing right in front of me, whoever that person may be. Call me mad, but I've found the solace I've been searching for. Sophie Heawood describes it thus: 'The older I get, the more I see how women are described as having gone mad, when what they've actually become is knowledgeable and powerful and fucking furious.'

I'm getting 'madder' by the day. If one thing living in the darkness of addiction for nearly twenty years has shown me, it's how bloody great it is living in the light. I get excited by a sausage sizzle! I have so much to look forward to.

I don't want to say I'll never relapse again, but I know I won't have a drink today. And I probably won't have one tomorrow either. Every day I wake up and vow not to drink. Every day I wake up with the same excitement I felt in that country-town motel with the heavy blue quilt the day after I performed sober for the first time. I know I can *live* sober now. Dogs bark, but they can be trained not to.

That training is an ongoing process, though. For my fifty-seventh birthday, my mum and sisters organised a high tea lunch for me in Adelaide. I was grateful they chose a non-alcoholic activity away from the temptation of a bar, but part of me still felt sorry for myself. Sitting at that table, laughing and reminiscing with my loved ones, I craved the feeling of a champagne flute in my hand. Drinking was so much fun, until it wasn't. Instead of submitting to my urge, I waited for it to pass. It lasted an hour. When I got home, I let myself be sad. I had a little cry, treated myself to a cigarette inside and watched Netflix until I fell asleep. The next morning, I vowed once again not to drink. And I didn't.

I've not spoken to my kids or family about my newfound solace. I feel like I need to practise what I preach. I don't want to tell them how well I'm doing; I want them to see it.

I've still not given up my dream of having my own sitcom or talk show, and I have even bigger aspirations of being a keynote speaker, getting back to London, New York and Los Angeles, and volunteering in a rehab-type centre to support my fellow alcoholics with the lessons I've learned. God knows I'd make a good lived-experience counsellor. I also want to do an extended tour of my show 'Gap Year', which I first performed in 2018 after *I'm a Celebrity*. That show really is the stage version of this book: it's my story, warts and all, from the coma to rehab and all the relapses in between. At the end of the show, I thank the audience for giving me my life back.

Since owning my alcoholism, I've had so many people tell me that I'm the reason they got clean and started going to recovery meetings. I spend time online daily talking to struggling alcoholics who've reached out to me, sharing the lessons I've learned and the things that have worked for me. There are so many alcoholics out there, alone and ashamed. I know what it feels like to be there; I've spent most of my life backed into the same dark corner. Helping others is a part of my recovery. It's step 12 of the 12-step program: *Having had a spiritual awakening as a result of these steps, we tried to carry this message to alcoholics and to practise these principles in all our affairs.*

It's at once freeing and sad to know that I'm not the only middle-aged woman battling this disease. The current statistics say that women are catching up to men in rates of alcohol consumption.[1] Stress has been blamed for an emerging rise in hazardous drinking among women in their forties and fifties,[2] and women aged fifty to seventy are more likely than younger women to consume alcohol at levels exceeding

1. Slade, Tim, Cath Chapman and Maree Teesson, 'Women's alcohol consumption catching up to men: why this matters,' National Drug and Alcohol Research Centre, October 25, 2016.
2. Fedele, Robert, 'Why Australian Women are Drinking More,' *Australian Nursing and Midwifery Journal*, July 16, 2019. https://anmj.org.au/why-australian-women-are-drinking-more-and-what-to-do-about-it/

national drinking guidelines.[3] Alcoholism is a progressive disease, so I'm not surprised that older women are the ones drinking to excess. I've seen women hit their forties, watch their kids leave home and fill the void with alcohol. The line between overdoing it at Friday night drinks and drinking vodka at breakfast is scarily thin. Trust me, I know.

It feels wonderful to be in a position where I can give back and share my hard-earned wisdom. But I know all too well, no one can be helped unless they want to be. Some people will happily drink themselves to death. I know a woman my age who has been an alcoholic for twenty-five years and has no plans to stop. She's got dedication, I'll give her that. This woman is married with two adult sons in professional jobs, and the boys and her husband just live with the drunk on the couch. They clean up around her and spray air freshener to mask the smell of stale alcohol. From where I sit, I can see she's suffering from terminal uniqueness. I used to have the same condition, thinking that my problems were so much worse than everyone else's, thinking I was special and above the rules because I *needed* two vodkas before a show, thinking no one

3. Hayes, Paul, '"It's normal": Older women and drinking at risky levels,' The Royal Australian College of General Practitioners, February 11, 2020. https://www1.racgp.org.au/newsgp/clinical/it-s-normal-older-women-and-drinking-at-risky-level

could ever understand what I was going through. It's a vicious cycle. You drink because you're sad, and you're sad because you drink and so on and so forth like a merry-go-round of self-pity. I finally feel like I've escaped the spinning carousel. I've stepped away from the revolving horses and the haunting carnival music and planted my feet on solid ground. I don't feel dizzy anymore.

Sue still lives next to the bungalow. When I visit her, it is a looming reminder of how far I've come and how hard I've fought. It's weird to think back on that time in my life, and even weirder to have ended up so close to my past, yet so far away. The healer doesn't live there anymore; I don't know where she is. As far as I can tell, the house is empty, except maybe for the rabbit, still shitting freely through the grotty rooms. There is a 'For Sale' sign out the front.

When Mary-Agnes sat on my bed at the Albert Road Clinic after my coma, she told me she knew I was going to have a happy ending. She was right. The born optimist of a born optimist. As I write this, my happy ending, Kasey Chambers' song 'I'm Alive' is playing in the background ...

CHAPTER 13

BRUTAL HONESTY

W HEN I SAT DOWN TO WRITE THIS BOOK, I HAD A two-word mantra: *brutal honesty*. I wanted to speak my truth, even when it hurt, even when I struggled to find the words, even when I couldn't see the computer screen for the tears. I have always mined my own human experience for material, but this time I wasn't looking for the punchline.

In 2011, I published my first memoir, *Me of the Never Never*, but that book concentrated mostly on the sunny side of the roads I have hiked. It hid the shadows, because I was determined to tell a joyous story. Every time I finished a chapter I would celebrate with a drink. No wonder it took me years to finish. *Me of the Never Never* was testament to the era I grew up in. I didn't dive beneath the surface much because I was still afraid of an awful lot. I'm not afraid anymore. This time, when I sat down at the table in my light-filled kitchen in Adelaide to write this book, I just wanted to tell my story – even the painful parts. It's been cathartic and exhausting and still surprisingly joyous.

Throughout my life I've pocketed seeds of knowledge and hope, and this book is the blooming garden. When I was living with my parents at age fifty-two, penniless and broken, my sister Emily told me I would write myself out of the internal hell I had created. I did. When I was in the depths of despair living in a drug den, the healer told me to hang on for my grandchildren. I did. When I saw my local GP in the middle of this relapse, he told me alcoholics die alone. That's a hard one to come to terms with. I don't need a sitcom romance anymore – I've got Netflix for that now – but I'm scared my heart will start calcifying if I don't open it up again. Here's hoping …

I've spent a lot of my life illuminating my childhood and looking for ways to pin my failings on my upbringing. Sure, my mum did yell at us, but who wouldn't with seven kids, no dishwasher and not a single moment to herself? You don't appreciate it as a kid and I was too busy to ever think about it until recently, but my mum is a strong, smart no-nonsense woman. She could have been a scientist or a doctor but the times meant she was a wife and a mother. She didn't have choices. I remember watching her sit in the car in the driveway after she'd done the grocery shopping, and I'd wonder what the hell she was doing. It was probably the only peace she got all week. When I had kids, I spent a lot of time sitting in the car in the driveway after doing the grocery shopping. I get it now, Mum, I get it.

The more I think about it, the more I understand the routine and the rigidity of my childhood. Maybe my parents had the right idea about raising kids: no elbows on the table, an 8 pm bedtime and a fun limit per day. God knows my free-range approach to parenting has had its pitfalls and literal falls: Tess fell through our bathroom skylight playing on the roof when she was a teenager.

Biddy tells a great joke, 'My mother is an alcoholic. And I use that term loosely … mother, that is.'

Jokes aside, I'm incredibly close to my kids, but I'm aware that our closeness borders on co-dependency. I have trouble saying no to them because of everything I've put them through. Having said that, they don't really need me in that way anymore.

But I'm forever grateful for the time I had with them. Before I became so sick I joke about what a free spirit I was. I was, but they had very strong boundaries at the start of their lives. I didn't abide whinging and no one ever laid hands on anyone else. You can lay down most of the groundwork in the first few years.

My kids are free-spirited, empathetic and excited about my future. They still don't blink an eye at my erraticism. They're creative, intuitive and have great taste in music. In my shit-mum schtick I joke about letting my kids climb on the roof when they were little, but they grew up with more freedom than I've ever known. Right or wrong, they've become incredible people after their time in the land of do as you please.

I remember a particularly unconventional weekend at the O'Loughlin house in Alice Springs when the kids were teenagers; it was after I'd come out as an alcoholic but before I'd separated from Chris. It was a Friday night and I'd gone out to pick up pizzas for dinner, but I was early so I went for a drive through The Gap area under the MacDonnell Ranges. An Indigenous woman ran onto the road in front of my car. I braked hard and jumped out of the car to yell at the two men who seemed to be chasing her. 'She's mad when she drinks,' they said, by way of explanation. I asked them where she lived and followed them. There was a sign on the window that read, 'This is a sober home,' and kids everywhere. I counted at least ten. The drunk woman's name was Cindy and I introduced myself to her mum, a woman in her seventies with skinny ankles and wrists. She looked crushed by the exhaustion of minding ten little kids and wrangling an alcoholic daughter in her twilight years. I looked at Cindy's mum and said, 'Do you want a break?' She hesitated. 'In my family, I'm her,' I said, pointing to Cindy, who gladly jumped in the front seat of my car. She had a can of VB beer in each cup of her bra.

When we pulled up in my driveway, I told Cindy, 'You can drink those here, but there's no alcohol allowed in my house. It'll kill me. Tonight, we're not going to drink. If I can do it, you can do it.' She finished her VBs in the car and we went inside, where she had a shower and went to bed in the girls' room in a clean set of clothes. In the morning, she washed her hair and got dressed in her washed and dried clothes from the day before. She looked like a new woman. 'I think I had a bit too much to drink last night,' she said on her way out the door. God I love alcoholics.

The next evening, the kids and I were watching a movie in the lounge room when we heard the loudest yelling. Chris caught a boy trying to steal a bike from our courtyard and marched him out the front of our premises shouting obscenities as he went. Mary-Agnes sat back down on the couch to continue watching the movie and said, 'Well, people are certainly getting a very mixed message coming over to our place this weekend.'

My kids have seen the best and worst of me. I was meant to be their safe harbour and I ended up being their storm. And, yet, they still love me. Mostly. It's like that tacky inspirational quote on Facebook: Sometimes your greatest contribution to this world isn't something you do, but rather, who you raise.

I returned to Alice Springs in July 2019 for Tess's thirtieth birthday. I stayed in a serviced apartment with my dear friend Mary-Anne in The Gap, across the road from the house I picked up Cindy from all those years ago. Going back to Alice is crushingly hard for me. I physically ache when I'm there. It's as though all my unhappy memories and shameful regrets come rushing back to me like the Todd River in flood.

We had a party for Tess at our house – sorry, Chris's house – with our closest friends and family. Walking through the French glass doors, everything was like it used to be. Well, almost. Chris was in the kitchen; he'd learned to cook since we separated. He'd also fixed the dry rot, fenced the backyard and installed ducted air-conditioning. My couch still had pride of place in the lounge room. I vividly remember fighting with Chris on the front lawn when the delivery driver dropped it off. How dare I buy something for the house without his permission? Twenty years later, it seems like a sound investment. I kept my observation to myself.

I walked through every room of the house and reminisced; the girls' bedroom where Cindy spent the night and woke up a new woman, the bathroom with the skylight Tess fell through, the laundry where I collapsed into a heap because all my clothes were wet and I needed to get on a flight in twenty minutes. I ran my hand over the smooth wood of our dining table, remembering all the nights we spent entertaining and laughing. We did have some good times. When I got to the door of the bedroom I shared with Chris, I paused, remembering all the nights we spent lying next to each other engulfed by darkness and silence. I couldn't go in.

I spent most of Tess's birthday party rolling around on the lounge room floor with Úna. Tickling my granddaughter's tummy surrounded by all my loved ones was one of those special moments in time when everything in the world feels right. All of my kids were happy, and we were together, in our home. I made eye contact with Chris and for the nth time I knew he would die for me and our kids. At dinner, I sat with Chris's sister Genevieve and we made each other laugh, like the good old days. I joked at the table, 'You know what, Chris, I think we should do another extension.' It was my way of taking my power back at the dining table that used to be mine, but no longer was.

The next night, Bert and his band, The Oh Balters, were playing at Monte's Lounge and we all went along. His cousin Charlie was in the band with him; they learned how to play guitar together in our lounge room when they were little. Now they were pulling crowds at pub gigs. I was glowing with pride.

I went to the gig with Mary-Anne and she told me she was going to have a few drinks. I felt the rope of my sobriety slacken slightly. When your chaperone gets drunk, you can get away with a lot more.

I tried to ignore the thought and went to chat with Henry. Years before, when Henry was younger than Mary is now, he moved back home to live and work in central Australia. Many times Henry and I would chat late into the night over a beer or three. I adore Henry's company as an adult, and I realise with a lurch in my heart how much I miss that connection with my eldest child. The rope of my sobriety loosened even more.

The pub was packed, and Chris was sitting in a booth all on his own, so I went and joined him. We chatted about nothing in particular and marvelled at having an adult son playing in a band at Monte's. Our conversation was light and familiar, until Chris let me know that he'd actually pre-booked the booth and his friends would arrive soon. It was brutal. It hurt more than all the insults we had traded over the years. I had to blink back tears as I got up to make room for his friends. I dropped the rope of my sobriety altogether.

When Biddy said she needed mascara, I offered to run to Coles to buy her some. I walked to the supermarket in a fit of sobbing tears and stopped by Liquorland on the way to get two mini bottles of vodka. I downed my old faithfuls and the rest of the night went by in a hazy blur. I added the gig to my bank of missing hours. I don't think anything disastrous happened, but it must have been obvious I was drunk. Everything was like it used to be: I was a messy drunk and everyone in Alice Springs knew it. I'd wanted to show them all that I'd changed, that I was in recovery, that I was better. But I wasn't.

On stage, Bert sang ...

I can see you step in time,
I have seen you walk the line.
I know when you'll tell a lie,
And when I'm on your mind.

Say you're in some trouble now,
And I'll be your man;
Say you need someone good.

The next morning, I woke up in the grotty serviced apartment in The Gap. Alice Springs had changed overnight, as only it can. The town turned from exciting and wonderful to severe and bleak. It was like a party at the end of the night, changing from fun to feral in the flash of a spilled drink or a raised fist or an unwelcome glance. The air was thick with the acrid scent of Gidgee bush. The usually stunning MacDonnell Ranges looked menacing in the harsh light of the day. The sun felt too hot for winter, and you know how I feel about the heat.

I could smell last night's vodka sweating out of my pores. I needed a drink like I needed oxygen. I waited for Mary-Anne to leave for brunch and ran barefoot to Pigglys Supermarket, the bitumen rough under my feet. When I arrived, panting, I realised I'd left my licence at the apartment, forgetting you need to show ID to buy grog in Alice. I could have screamed at my hopeless mind that's unable to remember my ID but knows all the words to Earl Spencer's speech from Princess Di's funeral. I raced back to the apartment, desperate for a sip of hard liquor and equally desperate not to get caught on my quest for a sip of said hard liquor. I prayed no one would recognise me. I was at once a household name, a mother and a fucking loser running barefoot through the streets of The Gap. If it wasn't so tragic, I would have laughed.

All I wanted was a hug from someone in my family, reassurance that everything was going to be okay, a reminder that I was more than my disease. I wrapped my arms around myself as I drank the vodka straight. Everyone knew I'd fallen off the wagon at Monte's Lounge, but they didn't know how tightly I'd been holding on before I dropped the rope of my sobriety. And I could hardly tell them now. When I flew back to Adelaide from Alice, I closed the aeroplane window shade so I couldn't see the red dirt turn to coastal shrubbery turn to urban sprawl.

I haven't been to Alice Springs since. I wonder how long it will take? I can't put myself through it again. I won't return until I know I'm strong enough to keep my head above the flood of sorrow that rages through me when I see the dry banks of the Todd River.

After twenty-seven years of marriage, five kids and eight years after separating, Chris and I have a respectful relationship. I have forgiven him – and myself – for the pain we put each other through, but I can't speak for him to tell you if he's done the same. We stay in touch about what the kids are up to and he messaged me recently to let me know one of our mutual friends in Alice had passed away. I'd love to have a proper conversation with him about our marriage, our respective failings and our happy memories. I reckon we'd have a lot to talk about. But at the moment I don't think we have enough distance. Healing takes time. And I am learning sometimes some words are safer left unspoken because words can't change the past.

*

An alcoholic's life is always full of regrets. My life is no exception. I regret hurting my family, putting myself in danger and destroying my career. I can't erase any of it, I know it's a part of me and a part of my story. I guess I felt powerless in my forties, in my thirties and even in my twenties. And when you are a kid you are completely powerless. Looking back, I can see the false strength vodka would give me. But that power wouldn't last and so I would relapse again and again and again. While I was fuelled by the first two mini bottles I would call my mother or my kids or my agent to reassure them I was okay, maybe I was also trying to convince myself, but that false belief was never sustained for more than an hour at best.

Every waking moment, sober or drunk, was a battle in my mind. The better days were often the worst. I knew that whatever happened, wherever I went, I would have to take 'me' with me. I was never good enough, never financially fit, never physically fit, never emotionally fit, I was never good enough in my own mind. I was filled with shame, remorse, self-loathing, self-pity, SELF, SELF, SELF. And I couldn't escape it. Someone wise once said you can never escape yourself. It took me fifty years to truly understand that. I would get news of great reviews or that my first book was being published, or that I had been invited to the Montreal Comedy Festival and where there should have been joy, there was just total despair. Anything that I could potentially look forward to was clouded by me. My obsession with what I believed was my inferior self was agonising and ugly and cut me off from the things I loved. Everything seemed unmanageable. Everything. Every drawer, every corner of my life, every corner of my mind. I let everything fall away. I didn't stand up for myself or stand up for any good in me. I retreated into a bottle. It was easier to devote myself to my pain and surrender, and I didn't know how to stop.

But here's the thing, finally in my mid-fifties I am changing it all. Nowadays I know how to fight, and I am starting to find the joy again. I am starting to acknowledge the things I am good at. Listening, babysitting, sharing. I'm learning that I can be great company around the dinner table without alcohol fuelling me. Finishing this book has helped me put a mirror up to myself. I haven't liked all of what it has revealed, but sharing my truth is powerful and means something. The waste of those years still haunts me, and it will always. But now I know that my dark can be someone else's light. That's what I want this book to be, a light. For others, and also for myself. Maybe words *don't* change the past, but when they are someone's truth they *absolutely* can change the future.

P.S.

Hey, everyone.

I feel like I am whispering, probably because I am. I am not supposed to be doing this. Still writing, that is. My publisher and I have had a happy tug of war over last-minute edits. And I'm now in overtime ... counting down to going to the printer. I'm in my Peter Alexander's (seriously, luxury is pockets in your pj's) and it's 3 am. I've decided that I've tossed and turned for the last time ever over what I should and shouldn't have said in this book. So here I am at my tiny table, happily giving it a shot to add that tiny bit more. Chances are these words won't make the book ... but what the heck.

This is what has been keeping me up at night. Two things.

1. Chris. I hope I have been fair. You can't make a life with someone, have kids and not have good times. I suddenly thought I hadn't said that properly, so I want to add my account of my happiest day and put it on the record. Chris and

I were in our mid-thirties and had a whole Sunday without the kids. We took Nick and my dear friend Lulu on a blind date. We headed out of town in a four-wheel drive, Chris and Nick were in the front and Lulu and I in the back. It was a winter wonderland Alice Springs day. We ended up at a table by ourselves at the Alice Springs Winery. The day was full of belly laughs and we had settled in to listen to a jazz band as the Centralian showcase of the setting sun had just begun. The MacDonnell Ranges was like a tourism ad with the changing shadows making them more and more striking by the second. Chris came back with a tray of drinks, leaned over to me and said, 'You look beautiful.' I did, I had just fake-tanned. But that feeling of the man I loved looking at me like that and smiling just at me. We all know those moments and those days ... For me that was one of the best days ever, and remembering it still makes me smile.

2. Catholicism. I hope I haven't betrayed my tribe by speaking so frankly about my feelings around this topic. Many people prayed for me to come out of my coma. Many of them were Catholic. Prayers came in thick and fast and I am so grateful for them, for that energy to be directed to my healing. Since the beginning of my battles my parents and my father-in-law were among the many who have prayed regularly for

me. I believe every prayer I was given was accounted for. I am now a huge believer in prayer, especially since I discovered that prayer is the final, crucial ingredient to my sobriety. My own newfound spirituality might not align with the Church, but I know I will be up to my neck in Catholics for the rest of my life and that suits me just fine. Some of the greatest people I know and have known are Catholic. Including clergy. Some of my best friends are Catholic!

P.P.S.

To my family, thank you to those of you who have read the manuscript for this book and given me feedback. And could someone also pass on to Mum and Dad that they don't have to feel obliged to read this book, just because I dedicated it to them. I mean I'm sure they have plenty of things to do and ... uhm ... that garden isn't going to water itself.

P.P.P.S.

I love you.

ACKNOWLEDGEMENTS

Thank you to the people who made this book a reality: my publisher Vanessa Radnidge at Hachette Australia, manager Sue Underwood, editors Claire de Medici and Sophie Mayfield and the team at Hachette Australia, and thanks also to my co-writer Alley Pascoe. Thank you also to booksellers and to readers. I hope my words help others feel hopeful for the future they can change. Finally, huge thanks to my family, who helped me tell this story.

RESOURCES

AUSTRALIA
National Alcohol and Other Drug Hotline
For free and confidential advice about alcohol and other drugs, call the National Alcohol and Other Drug Hotline, which will automatically direct you to the Alcohol and Drug Information Service in your state or territory. These local telephone services offer support, information, counselling and referral services.
1800 250 015

Lifeline
A 24-hour phone and online counselling service designed to help anyone through all problems.
www.lifeline.org.au
13 11 14

Sane
A helpline and website providing information and support for mental-health issues.
www.sane.org
1800 18 7263

Family Drug Support

A website and hotline offering information and support for families of drug and alcohol users, including a 24-hour support line.

www.fds.org.au

1300 368 186

NEW ZEALAND

Alcohol Drug Helpline

A website and 24-hour helpline offering free and confidential information, support and advice.

www.alcoholdrughelp.org.nz

0800 787 797

Lifeline

A 24-hour phone and text counselling service designed to help anyone through all problems.

www.lifeline.org.nz

0800 543 354

If you would like to find out more about Hachette Australia, our authors, upcoming events and new releases you can visit our website or our social media channels:

hachette.com.au

HachetteAustralia

HachetteAus